Quantum Quality reaffirms William Miller's reputation as one of the leading conceptual thinkers writing today for business leaders on the innovation process.

> W.E. Lambert
> Associate Human Resources Manager
> Health Care Sector
> The Procter & Gamble Company

Quantum Quality shows how new levels of quality and breakthrough results are possible by building on and going beyond principles of TQM.

> Dennis R. Fromholzer
> Executive Director, Strategy Development
> US WEST Communications

William Miller's *Quantum Quality* breaks new ground. It shows how the quality movement stands on the brink of transformation— from a mind-set of management based upon mistrust and fear . . . to one of empowerment, based on caring, individual responsibility and personal development.

> John Renesch
> Publisher
> **The New Leaders** business newsletter

QUANTUM
QUALITY

Quality
Improvement
through
Innovation,
Learning &
Creativity

QUANTUM QUALITY

Quality Improvement through Innovation, Learning & Creativity

WILLIAM C. MILLER

QUALITY RESOURCES
A Division of The Kraus Organization Limited

Most Quality Resources books are available at quantity discounts when purchased in bulk. For more information contact:

Special Sales Department
Quality Resources
A Division of The Kraus Organization Limited
One Water Street
White Plains, NY 10601
800-247-8519 914-761-9600

Printed in the United States of America
97 96 95 94 93 10 9 8 7 6 5 4 3 2 1

Quality Resources
A Division of The Kraus Organization Limited
One Water Street
White Plains, New York 10601
914-761-9600
800-247-8519

This book is also distributed by:

AMACOM Books, a division of
American Management Association
135 West 50th Street
New York, NY 10020

The paper used in this publication meets the minimum requirements of American National Standard for Information Sciences—Permanence of Paper for Printed Library Materials, ANSI Z39.48-1984.

Library of Congress Cataloging-in-Publication Data

Miller, William C. (William Cox), 1948–
    Quantum quality : quality improvement through innovation,
    learning, and creativity / William C. Miller
        p. cm.
    Includes index.
    ISBN 0-527-91719-2 (Quality Resources : acid free paper) :
    $19.95. — ISBN 0-8144-7851-4 (AMACOM : acid free paper)
    1. Total quality management. 2. Quality assurance. I. Title.
HD62.15.M55 1993
658.5′62—dc20   93-12408
                                                          CIP
ISBN 0-527-91719-2 (Quality Resources)
ISBN 0-8144-7851-4 (AMACOM Books)

*To fellow travelers
along this creative journey . . .*

*May the
quality of our work
always reflect the highest
quality of our souls.*

Acknowledgments

My heartfelt gratitude goes to the men and women who appear in this book for graciously granting me the time to interview them about their extraordinary successes in business:

Perry Gehring, DowElanco
Bob Galvin, Motorola
Fred Schwettman, Hewlett-Packard
Greg Watson, Xerox
Marie Clements, UNUM
Frank Carruba, Hewlett-Packard Laboratories
Cynthia Gaudet, UNUM
Linda Smith, Heller Financial
Joe Workland, PW Pipe
Emil Lojacano, LifeScan
Bill Lambert, Procter & Gamble
Jack Telnack, Ford
Ed McCracken, Silicon Graphics
Patricia Moore, Hewlett-Packard
Carlene Ellis, Intel
Suzanne Mamet, The Travelers
Mary Nelson, Bethel
Bob Vogenthaler, Procter & Gamble
Roger James
Chris Ehlers, Procter & Gamble
Bill Diana, Exxon
Gretchen Price, Procter & Gamble
Dennis Kekas, IBM
Rick Morris, IBM
Herman Maynard, DuPont
Frank Douglas, Marion Merrill Dow
Dick Eppel
Edgar Mitchell

In addition, for their ongoing encouragement and support of the work that culminated in this book, my gratitude goes to my wife, Kate Ludeman, my mother Mary Miller, and friends and colleagues including

John Adams, Jessica Fullmer, Mary Gelinas, Gerald Haman, L. A. Jordan, Bill Lambert, Rube Larson, Sue Lawson, Joel and Michelle Levy, Ed Quinn, John Renesch, Salina Spencer, Greg Watson, the staff at Quality Resources, plus Dave Ehler, Judy Robinson, John Sullivan, and the other wonderful folks at the Wilson Learning Corporation.

Contents

To the delight or consternation of managers and employees, a paradigm shift is occurring in the realm of quality improvement, surprisingly comparable to the shifts found in physics.

Emphases on technology, cost controls, or total quality are necessary yet insufficient to gain and maintain leadership in business. There's an inner game and an outer game of quality to be won.

Quantum Quality provides eight concrete ways to accelerate and enhance the quality improvement work already going on in most companies.

Only the driver of serving customers can carry a business to sustainable Baldrige-level quality and success. And Quantum Quality goes even beyond this in two ways.

We're being called upon to deal with turbulent, tough times in a mobilized and holistic frame of mind, to synthesize and find unity in diversity, rather than to attack and destroy.

We develop ourselves to make a stronger contribution to our work. And we use our work as a vehicle to develop ourselves. Then and only then do we get committed to our work.

Introduction:
"Living the Questions . . ."

All of us at one time or another face the need to make significant improvements in the way we get things done. Take Perry Gehring, for example. Perry is vice president of R&D for DowElanco, a joint venture of Dow Chemical and Eli Lilly corporations in agricultural chemical products. He recognized the need for more than just incremental improvement in the way research was conducted at his company. It was going to take a real breakthrough in process improvement, stakeholder benefit, and in personal commitment to quality.

For Perry's research group, their product development process can easily take 7–10 years, passing through three phases. The first is the discovery phase, in which the activity and efficacy of chemical compounds are examined. Then, in the predevelopment phase, the efficacy, commercial potential, and likelihood of obtaining required registrations for using the product are evaluated.

> *Side-by-side field trials using competitive products as benchmarks are conducted to assess efficacy. Registerability is assessed from extensive studies of the health and environmental properties. This cycle requires 3 years and costs from $5–10 million per year per compound.*
>
> *If the potential product survives this, it moves to the development phase, which also requires 3 years and is even more expensive. It involves larger numbers of research and development personnel around the globe. Manufacturing also needs to build plants to produce increasing amounts up to commercial quantities. Because the huge costs of the development phase, we want to be 99.9 percent sure that the compound will be commercially successful before we put it into development. And currently our goal is to be 50 percent sure before we put it into predevelopment.*

In a competitive business such as DowElanco's, this assessment must be done quickly. If more than two years are required for the discovery phase, it is likely that they might never catch up. In the early 1980s, it was taking 4–5 years to make the decision to put a compound into predevelopment. Too many potential products were failing late in the development cycle.

> *Having decided that no failures of a potential product should occur in the development phase, we focused on predevelopment. To assess efficacy and*

commercial potential on a global basis, we needed to use standard experimental designs for field studies with a very specific, well-understood objective. This required training of selected researchers globally—and more important, their buy-in and commitment. This did not occur overnight.

To evaluate potential adverse health and environmental effects in predevelopment, studies needed to be started earlier. To spend large amounts of resources on this prior to a complete evaluation of the value of the potential product was difficult to accept. To accept these types of changes in paradigm required a recognition that the expense associated with 50 percent failure was large, but it would be even larger if the failure occurred later.

This evolution also necessitated a much more rigorous late-stage discovery research process, and even earlier.

In this more rigorous system, the issue is often raised whether scientists have enough freedom to be creative.

Few scientists desire to invent a technical success that has too little value to justify development and use. When people understand the needs at the end of the process, they generally do a good job managing their efforts. They seek their own critical assessment and peer review of their endeavors. In our company, product goals are selected using teams composed of both technical and commercial personnel. This helps to create understanding and buy-in by our scientists. What I have described was and continues to be far from simple. It requires breakthroughs not only in technology, but also in the management of the R&D process. Often, buy-in to the latter is more difficult than the former.

This process-improvement effort has had a dramatic impact on the timeliness and accuracy of choosing the right products to move on to the development phase.

We're making some headway. In 1984, it was requiring of us anywhere from 4–5 years in the field just to make the decision to put a compound in development. We now do that in 1 to 1.5 years.

AND right now, we have a problem in that none of our materials in predevelopment are failing. It's a wonderful, terrible problem to have, because it's so costly to have things in development. But none of our recommendations are failing.

Perry Gehring is just one of many, many people who recognize the need for making more than just incremental improvements if we are going to have sustainable growth in our companies and in our people. Neither Perry nor the others you will meet in this book pretend that they alone are responsible for producing dramatic leaps forward; it's a group effort. But these people have perhaps learned and achieved more than most. How they have accomplished this deserves recognition and elaboration.

Indeed, the people whose words you will read here are all practicing principles of innovation and quality improvement that go beyond how we typically implement total quality management (TQM). I am pleased to be able to present this platform for Perry and others to tell their stories, as they demonstrate new principles for achieving higher levels of success and personal satisfaction—producing not only corporate growth, but also personal growth.

In June 1991, I received a call from Quality Resources, the publisher of this book, inquiring about a book proposal I was working on that linked quality improvement and creativity. (Quality Resources had previously published books on quality by Ishikawa and Taguchi, among others.) They were interested in a book that explored the fundamental paradigm changes that were emerging in the quality movement, both in the United States and around the world.

This book is the result of exploring our mutual interests. There is indeed an emerging, fundamental shift in the mind-set, tools, and management of quality improvement—a shift as substantial as the progressive transformation from quality control (QC) to quality assurance (QA) to total quality management (TQM). The term that many have begun to use to describe this new transformation is Quantum Quality (QQ), which includes and yet expands on QC, QA, and TQM.

Just what might be missing from current quality improvement practices? What's the need that Quantum Quality is emerging to fill? Perhaps you've observed some of the following:

- A strong emphasis on measurement and meeting customer requirements, yet getting "bogged down" or making only incremental improvements without breakthroughs (see Chapter One)

- An imbalance between analysis and creativity in defining actual improvements, or an imbalance between speed and sustainability (see Chapter Two)

- A proliferation of quality improvement processes that address only the intellectual, not emotional, aspects of effective process improvement (see chapters Three and Twelve)

- Profit and cost motivations seemingly at odds with making the improvements that optimize customer and supplier relationships (see Chapter Four)

- Hesitancy to take risks or to understand and continually adjust to changing business conditions (see Chapter Five)

- Quality training programs that are perceived (and resisted) as ways to "fix" or control employees' behavior, rather than an effective means to develop spirit, skills, commitment, and security (see Chapter Six)

- Not analyzing situations from enough of a "systems" perspective (even when cross-functional teams are involved)—especially in managing the corporate culture for quality (see Chapter Seven)

- Getting caught in "quick fix" or "group think" during brainstorming sessions, limiting the ideas to either only incremental or only "blue sky" ideas (see Chapter Eight)

- Taking too long to make decisions (slow cycle time), and getting only compliance rather than commitment to decisions (see Chapter Nine)

- Getting bogged down during implementation, due to resistance to change or a lack of leadership or managership at different levels of the organization (see Chapter Ten)

- Appraising only tangible results and not the "transferable learning" or risk-taking in quality efforts; emphasizing tangible rewards to the exclusion of intrinsic satisfactions (see Chapter Eleven)

- Focusing only on the technical side of quality, not the personal values that make quality a deeply personal way of living and growing (see Chapter Twelve)

For example, let's consider the hesitancy to take risks or to understand and continually adjust to changing business conditions (see Chapter Five). The renaissance in quality at Motorola had an auspicious beginning in the early 1980s. At an elaborate 3-day conference with all the top executives celebrating the past year's success, Bob Galvin (chairman of the executive committee to the board of directors) asked if anyone wanted to say something before the final closing. Art Sundry, head of the C&E (communication and electronics) sales organization, stood up, simply stated, "Our quality stinks," and sat down. The group was stunned. Bob called Art to his office the next day, not to berate him but to inquire what he meant and why. The outcome of their discussion was a study of customer perceptions of Motorola quality—and ultimately the improvements that won Motorola the first Baldrige Award.

Without Art's courage, the course of Motorola's history and success might have been very different. And without Bob's openness to inquiring about how customers might be perceiving their products differently (perhaps from new expectations or changing needs), the episode could have ended with a reprimand rather than a Baldrige. They both represent extraordinary models of people who can shift their thinking (and their emotions) to do what's best in an uncertain business situation.

To understand this shift in thinking that's required for managing uncertainty, it's helpful to go back to the pre-1900s when the industrial age began to flourish. At that time, most goods were shipped by land—by wagons, trains, or (later) trucks. You could learn from your map how you would arrive at your chosen destination—the routes were basically finite and fixed. As long as the roads remained open, and the vehicle was kept under control with no breakdowns, you could drive on and eventually arrive.

For most of this century, our concepts of management have followed a "driving" model: pick a goal (destination), learn about the conditions (along the routes), set a plan, and then carefully follow the plan. With controls in place to minimize errors in implementing the plan, you would arrive safely. Traditional management-by-objectives (MBO) was based on this model, as is most forecast-based strategic planning.

This model of management, which I call *strategic road-mapping*, is aimed at minimizing risk. Learning happens once, at the beginning. Plans are set and followed with strict controls as much as possible. This works if the business environment remains relatively stable, and there are no breakdowns or loss of control. But that's an "if" that can't be counted on anymore!

This "driving" model of managing a business doesn't suit the world of post-industrial, information-age business. Change happens too fast, with frequent discontinuities in economic, technological, social and political life. It's like driving through an earthquake-prone swamp, with shifting sands, in a storm; the environment is not stable, leading to unreliable pathways, breakdowns, and loss of control.

In this information age, managing a business is more like flying in turbulent weather. Pilots arrive at their destinations only if they continuously learn about the environment and make continuous mid-course corrections. (For example, a flight from San Francisco to Tokyo is at least slightly off course 95 percent of the time.)

This model of management, which I call *strategic compassing*, aims at managing uncertainty rather than minimizing risk. It is based on continuous learning and improvement. By comparison, strategic road-mapping is really short-term, tactical planning, rather than long-term strategic positioning. It's based on one-time learning and the controlled implementation of a one-time plan.

To win in these turbulent times of transnational corporations and global competition, we must emphasize the *continuous learning and high-impact improvement* that is fundamental to Quantum Quality.

Quantum Quality is just emerging as a new paradigm, and there is still much to uncover about this next stage of working smarter, richer, better, healthier. As with any new paradigm of thought involving a favorite topic, the new principles and dimensions will be agreed to by some and disputed by others. Any new paradigm emerges slowly, through inquiry and dialogue. Thus, as you read this book, I expect that you may welcome some statements, but argue with others.

If such a dialogue takes place, the book will be doing its job. The purpose of this book is to introduce a framework for understanding this new paradigm of quality—to frame the questions of that dialogue and to provide concrete, practical descriptions of how people in companies everywhere are implementing a broader set of principles and achieving breakthrough levels of success in process improvement, stakeholder benefit, and personal commitment to excellence.

Indeed, the people you will meet in this book are evidence that Quantum Quality is already at work in corporate life. So the questions become: What are the dimensions of this new paradigm called Quantum Quality? What are the key principles that make up a QQ mindset? What are some of the practical, day-to-day practices and tools for implementing QQ? What are the means to manage and institutionalize an alignment between the individuals and teams who implement QQ and the sponsoring managers who set up the culture for quality?

The answers to those questions are just beginning to emerge. This book is a first step in providing a firm foundation in the dimensions, mindset, and essence of Quantum Quality:

Part I. The Dimensions of Quantum Quality

Chapter One. Quantum Quality—The New Paradigm
Chapter Two. Working Smarter, Richer, Better, Healthier
Chapter Three. Success Is a Journey, Not a Destination

Part II. The Mind-Set of Quantum Quality

Chapter Four. Set Goals Beyond Self-Interest
Chapter Five. Manage Uncertainty Rather than Minimize Risk

Chapter Six. Make Employee Development a Two-Way Street
Chapter Seven. Analyze Issues from a "Systems" Perspective
Chapter Eight. Use Four Distinct Strategies to Find Creative Options
Chapter Nine. Reach Speedy Decisions, Based on Group Values
Chapter Ten. Assume Leadership and Managership at All Levels
Chapter Eleven. Reward Focused Learning as Well as Improvement

Part III. The Essence of Quantum Quality

Chapter Twelve. Putting Our Deepest Values to Work

Each of the chapters in Part II on the mind-set contains three sections:

- *Mastering the Mind-Set,* with a significant case example.
- *Strengthening the System,* showing which organizational systems can help to "institutionalize" the mind-set.
- *Practicing the Paradigm,* linking the principles of the mind-set to the basic dimensions of QQ.

One of the key features of this book is what I call Strategic Innovation Management™. It is a comprehensive, prescriptive model of what distinct issues need to be addressed to manage teams through distinct stages of the quality process. As a framework for building a corporate culture that fosters quality and innovation, it is shown in Chapter Seven, after enough groundwork has been laid to make it easy to work with.

Although this book provides many inspiring stories of achieving quantum leaps, and much practical advice, you as the reader are still largely on your own in applying Quantum Quality to your own unique work circumstances. It will require a major shift in how we learn and act for quality improvement. Some of us tend to focus on the process of learning and may fail to take action on what we've learned, and thus not achieve *results*. Others of us love to *do*, to be action-oriented, and concentrate on tangible end *results* while neglecting the *process* of getting there.

For doers, a key to exploring the new paradigm of Quantum Quality is to learn to "live with (or dwell on) the questions" rather than finalize the answers: Use this book to get "answers for now," but keep looking for newer, better answers to emerge. This will stimulate continuous learning—and yet it goes against the grain of how we were taught to always have the "right" answer. However, in a rapidly changing world, the "right" answer remains so for an ever-shorter period of time.

For learners, the key is to *work with* or *apply* the answers for now, rather than gathering more and more information: Use this book to generate creative solutions to issues; then use the results to gain valuable experience and stimulation for further inquiry.

"Living with the questions" promotes continuous learning. "Working with the answers for now" promotes continuous improvements—both breakthrough and incremental. And as with any new paradigm, further clarity will unfold over time. It all depends on how well we carry on a heartfelt dialogue and live with the questions. In this light, perhaps the greatest value from this book will be the questions it raises and seeks to address in addition to the specific answers for now it provides.

Quantum Quality can thus give you that extra, creative edge for quality that one needs to win in the 1990s. Although there may not be a single company that practices *all* the principles of Quantum Quality, each of the following chapters emphasizes one example of a company successfully practicing one of the principles. It is hoped that you can use their stories to stimulate your own efforts to put Quantum Quality into action and achieve your own story of success, achieving leaps in work processes, customer impact, and personal commitment.

*   *   *

To help shape the future of quality improvement, I encourage your active participation in the dialogue that is this book. If you wish to correspond with me, please feel free to write me care of the publisher.

PART 1

The Dimensions of Quantum Quality

1

Quantum Quality— The New Paradigm

We had an organization that was committed to total quality control. Management supported it, and we sent groups of people off to class to learn how to use the TQC tools to solve problems, with some impressive results. I remember very vividly one team which in 3 months was able to save almost $1 million a year just on the maintenance of one piece of "clean room" equipment.

Then I noticed that over time, there were less and less teams going, and the results were becoming less and less impressive.

—Fred Schwettman, vice president and general manager, Hewlett-Packard Corp., Circuit Technology Division

Hewlett-Packard (HP) is one of the most respected companies in the United States both for the quality of its products and for its traditions of employee care and involvement. Yet even at Hewlett-Packard, quality improvement is entering into a new era. When it comes to quality improvement, it's not a matter of just doing things better. It's doing them differently.

The Circuit Technology Division is a $400 million per year business that designs, builds, and manufactures integrated circuits and printed circuit boards for HP. It supplies about 90 percent of the company's market needs, operating plants in the United States, Germany, Scotland, and Singapore .

People were really unhappy with the current state. We weren't doing what we needed to get done. We had a big meeting and we got into this discussion about quality. There was this sort of a groundswell and all of the sudden, people were saying, well, now, let's really get in and do it right this time.

3

Overall, the challenge was, "How will a group of managers take on and embrace quality at a different level of skill and a different level of commitment than before?" To focus on this, ten of their best functional managers and one general manager left their line jobs and took a careful, full-time look at what the industry and the rest of the world were doing in terms of quality. They concluded that some key things would have to be very different from what had gone before to pull the Circuit Technology Division toward the future.

> *One of the first things was to adopt a process used at Xerox called LUTI: Learn, Use, Teach and Inspect. We felt this was the highest priority because the hypothesis of why the previous effort was fading was that management was not practicing what we were preaching; after a while people would conclude that if it's not important enough for managers to do it then obviously it's not important for them.*
>
> *They put together a one week training class for managers. The thing about the Xerox process was that we think it really addressed two main issues. One was that management was really going to participate and learn and then the second thing was that they were going to use the tools. We developed a certification process so even after you were trained with the class you had to use a project; you had to show uses of tools and then you became certified. In about a year and a half and at this point I think we have about 2,800 out of 3,500 management-level people trained.*

Whenever managers have a project or problem, they are applying a standard way to find creative options or solutions. The transition to this turned out to be difficult because they had all spent the last 30 years learning to do things one way, and now it was time to do them another way.

> *The things that have been most dramatic is the quality of meetings—the time, savings and the enthusiasm of people. We've gotten away from a lot of the agendas that are at cross-purposes at meetings. What I've observed is that people are applying their energy to the issue, not to what the answer is, not to their own ideas. The whole idea of synergy is to get more out of the team than just the sum of the individuals.*
>
> *The results are going to take a while. The hard and fast financial results and things like that, I think, take a lot longer because there is a whole organization that has to get lined up and working on the problems.*

What's new about what Fred Schwettman and his colleagues are doing? Certainly, one of the key success factors that will help sustain this energy is the fact that the core team really embodied quality. They were true role models. They showed by their behavior the effectiveness of what they recommended to everyone else.

But there's more to it than that. Quality-improvement efforts are undergoing a major evolution—or revolution. Perhaps, surprisingly, the historical development of modern physics can gives us a proper perspective for understanding what's new and different in the quality arena.

Over 400 years ago, when Copernicus presented his findings on the orbital nature of the solar system, he was accused of religious heresy: Everyone "knew" that the stars and planets revolved around the earth, not the other way around as Copernicus claimed. His observations and calculations formed the modern science of physics.

Two hundred years later, Isaac Newton formulated his laws of motion. His equations described our everyday "common sense" reality so well that his theories were considered unsurpassable.

But in the late 1800s, some phenomena were observed (regarding light) that were difficult to explain using Newton's laws. Albert Einstein formulated his theory of relativity, which explained the observations without negating Newton's work: It simply stated Newton was right if relative speeds were slow enough, but there was a more encompassing law of nature.

Then, in the first half of the twentieth century, some other phenomena were observed (regarding nuclear activity) that were difficult to explain using only Einstein's notions. Werner Heisenberg and others formulated the equations and "philosophy" of quantum mechanics. The new theory didn't negate Einstein's or Newton's work: It again simply stated there was an envelope of understanding that included—but surpassed—each of these two pioneer's great work.[1]

The transformation "including but surpassing" existing theories and models of physics is illustrated in Figure 1.1. Each of these developments represents a shift in our mental model of the nature of the universe (and our place in it). Each of these mental models is a "paradigm"—a basic way of perceiving and understanding the world.

Our patterns of thinking and perceiving exist within some paradigm as fish exist within water: All our thoughts are filtered through this fundamental way of moving in and interpreting the world. A paradigm is usually taken for granted as "reality"—"That's just the way things are; any other notion is foolishness."

---

[1] Interestingly, Einstein resisted the emergence of this new paradigm. He objected to Heisenberg's "probability" theory by saying, "God does not play dice!"

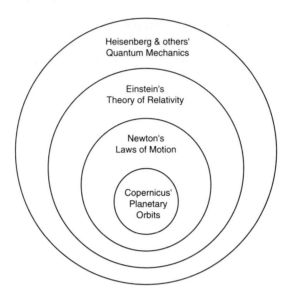

FIGURE 1.1.   Paradigm Changes in Physics

Paradigms are so fundamental to knowing how to operate securely in the world that any change to a paradigm can be felt as dramatically exciting or threatening. Paradigm shifts impact our understanding of ourselves, our sense of competence in the world ("Do I understand how to be successful in this new world?"), and our self-esteem.

And, to the delight or consternation of managers and employees, a paradigm shift is occurring today in the realm of **quality improvement**, *comparable to the shifts found in physics.*

In the early 1900s, Frederick Taylor led early efforts to control production quality. The first period emphasized *quality control* (QC). The dimensions of this paradigm were (1) inspection and (2) measurement of results. The definition of "quality" that most characterizes this paradigm is *quality is the absence of variation in output.*

The second phase, influenced strongly by Walter Shewhart, emerged as *quality assurance* (QA). The dimensions of this paradigm were (1) statistical analysis (via statistical quality control, which has evolved into statistical process control), to focus on problem definition; and (2) process improvement (with Shewhart's Plan–Do–Check–Act model).[2] QA provides more of a systematic, prevention-based approach to quality than

---

[2] The first two are most typical of QC; the latter two are the contribution of QA.

QC. The definition of "quality" that most characterizes this paradigm is *quality is conformance to high standards.*

Whole departments became devoted to these two activities. As noted by John C. Day, DuPont's manager of world class manufacturing, when excellence was measured by lack of defects, the standard approach was to add more inspection steps.[3]

In a story that has been well documented, the work of W. Edwards Deming and Joseph Juran in Japan helped to give birth to a more "Einsteinian" understanding of quality—known as *total quality management* (TQM), or sometimes, *continuous improvement* (CI). The dimensions that define the paradigm of TQM have primarily been (1) employee empowerment, (2) team accountability, (3) customer–supplier focus, and (4) speed (including cycle-time reduction). These dimensions took TQM beyond QC and QA to frame TQM's more powerful contribution to business success.

Using a whole array of tools for problem analysis (e.g., fishbone diagrams), developed by Ishikawa and other quality leaders, TQM is now a full-blown "movement" around the world. It focuses much more on the *users* of a product or service. For example, the definition used at Compaq Computers is "quality is the value of Compaq's products and services as perceived by our customers"—a definition that includes and yet surpasses the notion of "conformance to high standards." According to the TQM paradigm, *quality is successfully meeting internal and external customer expectations.*

Total quality management has become deservedly popular in the last 10-15 years, leading to many extraordinary turnarounds in business. The Xerox Corporation is rightly identified as one of the most successful companies in putting TQM to work in order to have a significant impact on their business results and reputation. The reasons for Xerox's success are described by Xerox's Greg Watson, vice president of quality, Office Document Product Division:

> *At Xerox, the strength of the quality system may be described in terms of a few key enablers. First is leadership. David Kearns did an exceptional job in personally explaining and demonstrating his commitment to quality. For example, he personally led the Leadership Through Quality training for his staff group and continued his emphasis by asking the kinds of questions that demonstrated his continuing commitment to quality. The second key enabler was on teamwork or Team Xerox. Xerox maintained consistent follow-*

---

[3] "The Quality Imperative," *Business Week*, Oct. 25, 1991, pp. 10, 14.

through beyond the slogan by emphasizing cross-functional teams, quality improvement teams, as well as work group teamwork. The third enabler was that Xerox taught everybody a simple process for problem solving and quality improvement—then they trained their managers to facilitate that process. Fourth, they used benchmarking, to identify a standard of comparison which would challenge them with both a goal for improvement and an example of another comany which had out-performed Xerox in a particular process area. Benchmarking is a continuous learning process whereby they not only set a goal in terms of the magnitude of performance that indicates "world class," but they have examples of what enabled that other company to create that level of performance.

What Xerox did not do back then was implement a lot of statistical programs. They focused on statistical process control (SPC), but they limited this focus to manufacturing. SPC is elegant as a control approach for transaction-intensive processes, but it is not appropriate for every process. If you were to implement a QC system for an entire business with SPC, then you would have applications in marketing, sales, distribution, accounting, patent applications, etc. Not all of these processes require the same degree of statistical treatment for an effective control system. There is a tendency to make the process more complex than it needs to be.

One important limitation found in so many corporate programs on TQM and continuous improvement is the emphasis on *incremental improvement*. These companies are beginning to "hit the wall"—not getting the full impact and competitive benefit from their quality efforts. They are looking for something more, even as skeptics have begun writing about the failure of TQM to deliver sufficient results.

At Alcoa, for example, chairman Paul H. O'Neill recently eliminated Alcoa's 10-year-old "continuous improvement" program, calling it a "major mistake" because it was producing only incremental improvements, whereas he wanted "quantum improvement." His staff at Alcoa had benchmarked the company against its competitors and came up short, so O'Neill set goals to close the gap by 80% within 2 years. By raising its yield of good-quality aluminum for beverage cans by 15%, Alcoa could possibly raise its per-share earnings by $1.[4]

It is not that TQM has poor tools or values. They're excellent. They're also potentially much more effective than the results people have produced with them! It's just that the context in which people are perceiving

---

[4] "The Quality Imperative," op. cit., p. 14.

and applying them is not inclusive enough. A newer, broader context is needed. To get that extra something, that quantum improvement, a new "envelope" of understanding is needed—a new paradigm for quality that embraces yet expands beyond the concepts and tools of quality assurance and TQM, in the same way that quantum mechanics included but surpassed the laws of motion and the theory of relativity.

A term for this new paradigm that has been floating around since 1990 is Quantum Quality (QQ). I first heard the term Quantum Quality from Paul Elsner, head of the Mariposa Community College District in Arizona, one of the most progressive and successful systems in America. He used the term in a specific way: a breakthrough in personal motivation, commitment, and initiative toward quality. The chairman of Alcoa used the term to mean a jump in quality results.

Overall, Quantum Quality denotes the process of making the leap from one, existing level of quality to another—in any of three ways:

1. A leap in *work processes*—substantially transforming the way work is done. These breakthroughs can be either of a "technical" or a "personal" kind:
   - Technical—"No one has ever been able to do this before."
   - Personal—"I/we have never done this before" (even if others have).
2. A leap in *stakeholder benefit*—producing dramatic results in serving customers and other stakeholders, whether from a revolutionary change or the accumulation of incremental, evolutionary changes. Here, the value produced for a customer is the breakthrough.
3. A leap in *personal and team commitment*—making "quality" a personal way of life (even beyond work) that reflects one's dedication to basic human values such as caring and integrity.

Therefore, in this "quantum" paradigm, *quality is the achievement of significant leaps in work processes, stakeholder benefit, and personal commitment—based on values of caring and integrity.*[5]

As we shall explore later in this chapter and in the next, the dimensions of this paradigm are (1) learning, (2) values, (3) creativity, and (4) sustainability. As Figure 1.2 indicates, the dimensions of QA and TQM are included—quite deliberately (and enthusiastically)—within the QQ paradigm.

---

[5] By "integrity," I mean the alignment and congruence of what a person believes, says, and does—thought, word, and deed. See Chapter Four.

Forming a "community" feeling, a close relationship, between supplier and customer is the key issue in the way top companies have chosen to do business with only "cream of the crop" suppliers. After Motorola won the Baldrige Award in 1988, it told its 3600 largest suppliers that they too must compete for the award. 200 refused and were dropped. Xerox eliminated 90% of its suppliers between 1982 and 1988; the percent of defect-free components from suppliers rose from 92% to 99.97%. Ford has reduced its suppliers from 50,000 to 10,000 between the 1970s and 1990s. This is more than just picking the best suppliers. As Arthur Tenner and Irving DeToro state in *Total Quality Management*:

> *It is based on partnerships and interdependence between the corporations and their select suppliers. It includes an investment in training and a trust in the sharing of data. Prompt, collaborative problems solving might replace finger pointing and abandonment. Inventory planning and reduction can be managed jointly between the customer and the supplier. Development of future products and services will justify involving key suppliers earlier in the planning stage. Better planning will favor longer-term decision making and help to break down barriers that inhibit joint research and development.[6]*

Quantum Quality endorses the use of the tools and methodologies of quality assurance and TQM. It is "simply" the next envelope for making use of those tools—and the new tools that will emerge from QQ— involving a deeper, more dynamic understanding of the nature of quality and sustainable growth in today's world.

One example of the shift in thinking from TQM to QQ is the new relationship to customers. A major contribution of TQM to business practices over the past 10–15 years has been the focus of quality on "meeting customer needs." But, today, a new term is making the rounds in companies such as IBM, Procter & Gamble, and Johnson & Johnson: "delighting the customer." This is one of the first times that a word suggesting an *emotion* has appeared in the quality-improvement vocabulary—note the "emotional" tone replacing a more technical definition. Greg Watson puts this evolution in proper perspective:

> *For some, the definition of quality is conformance to customer requirements. The only standard of quality for them is "zero defects" against that definition. That approach is not sufficient for quality in today's business environment because it requires the customer to declare exactly what they want—even*

---

[6] Arthur Tenner and Irving DeToro, *Total Quality Management* (Boston: Addison-Wesley, 1992), p. 199–200.

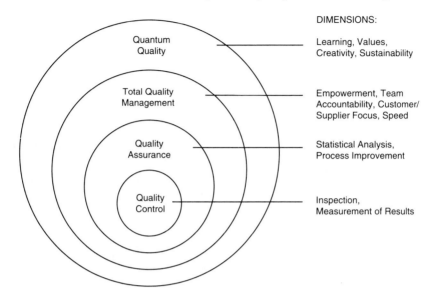

DIMENSIONS:

Quantum Quality — Learning, Values, Creativity, Sustainability

Total Quality Management — Empowerment, Team Accountability, Customer/ Supplier Focus, Speed

Quality Assurance — Statistical Analysis, Process Improvement

Quality Control — Inspection, Measurement of Results

FIGURE 1.2.   Paradigm Changes in Quality

when they are not able to precisely define their need. The relationship that you ought to seek with your customer is one where your customer is like one of your closest friends. You make yourself available for your friends, recognizing what is important for them—you're able to get out of your own personal perspective and understand things from their perspective. Otherwise, all you're doing is relating to them more impersonally and they have to tell you what they think and feel—that's more like a relationship with an acquaintance or a stranger.

The sales organization in most companies recognize that the sales process is about relationships. Some professionals even say that the three most important aspects of sales are relationships, relationships, relationships! The sales and customer service processes can teach a lot about what people need to deliver in order to satisfy the customer. These processes are where the key touchpoints exist with customers. Quality needs to be built into these processes. It the quality community in a company doesn't focus on that development, then I think, they are missing a key process point.

As a new paradigm, Quantum Quality will grow to have its own unique dimensions, mind-set, principles, and management issues. As an example of the new direction for management and corporate culture, Greg Watson has this to say:

If you go back to Alan Kennedy's earlier works on corporate culture, you'll see that he was defining a limited concept of corporate culture.[7] In other words, it did not fit the quality paradigm, because the quality paradigm extends beyond the internal organizational structure to include both suppliers and customers. If you expand corporate culture to include both suppliers and customers, then you are really emphasizing a sense of community.

This sense of community links together with Genichi Taguchi's concept of quality.[8] Taguchi talks about quality as what is good for society. He said that quality minimizes the cost to society for products and services. In other words, the whole system must be considered as a total cost of ownership in order to truly evaluate quality. If you are creating scrap at your supplier or making an environmental hazard by creating waste there instead of at your own facility, it has not done any good—it has merely transferred the problem someplace else and forced someone else to deal with the inefficiency or ineffectiveness. Or, if you are creating a problem for your customer because your product is not environmentally disposable, then you're not doing society any good. Somebody will pay the cost of disposal, even if it doesn't show on your own company's financial statements.

Taguchi's theories culminate in R&D issues about product design. As you start looking at where the quality movement is going, you see more and more emphasis on the design phase of product development. As a matter of fact, in my organization over half of the people work on design quality. That's the major thrust, I think, for the future. So, we've reached the point where the innovation process is a fundamental quality process, no matter what else you do!

Greg's concluding comment on the innovation process is quite significant, because QQ is virtually identical with innovation in its style of thinking and managing.

Innovation has been defined in somewhat contradictory terms. In Masaaki Imai's book *Kaizen*, innovation is contrasted with incremental improvement and applied narrowly to breakthrough production methods only.[9] Most TQM practitioners, including Baldrige Award professionals,

---

[7] See, e.g., Terrence E. Deal and Allan A. Kennedy, *Corporate Cultures: The Rites and Rituals of Corporate Life* (Reading, MA: Addison-Wesley, 1984).

[8] Genichi Taguchi, *Introduction to Quality Engineering: Designing Quality into Products and Processes* (Tokyo: Asian Productivity Association, 1986). See also Robert H. Lochner and Joseph E. Matar, *Designing for Quality: An Introduction to the Best of Taguchi and Western Methods of Statistical Experimental Design* (White Plains, NY: Quality Resources, 1990).

[9] Masaaki Imai, *Kaizen: The Key to Japan's Competitive Success* (New York: Random House, 1986).

typically refer to innovation as breakthroughs. However, in a study of new product breakthroughs conducted by the Arthur D. Little consulting firm, innovation meant just the opposite: It refers to incremental improvements in product lines, and contrasts with fundamental product breakthroughs.

Thus, for some, innovation means breakthrough solutions; for others, innovation means incremental improvements. I would propose that *innovation is both*.

And, likewise, quality improvement must be just as broadly conceived *and practiced*. The term "continuous improvement" has been too narrowly viewed as incremental improvement. As shown in Figure 1.3, what truly needs to be continuous over time is the entire cycle of leaps and incremental changes. Otherwise, we will be caught either (a) ignoring opportunities for small, impactful changes or (b) missing opportunities for substantive change when a process has reached its limit of effectiveness.

Greg Watson provides one way that these two play together in the most successful organizations.

There are two levels that an organization works at simultaneously. One level is the daily process management of the business fundamentals—what is going on in the trenches on a day-to-day basis. This is where you want to

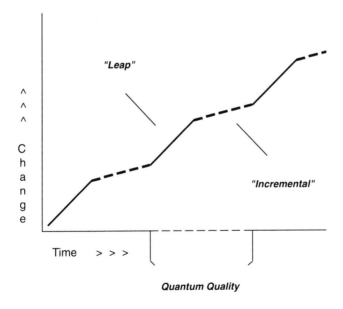

FIGURE 1.3. Innovation and Change

emphasize quality control, standardization, and kaizen or continuous improvement. The second level is a more strategic plane where breakthrough improvements are desired. What you want in strategic area are organizational designs, and process challenges that require new paradigms and ways of looking at things so that your people stay excited and your business stays ahead.

This strategic focus is one of the reasons that Hewlett-Packard has been so good over the years in being able to adapt. HP has taken an approach, led by John Young, their CEO, to attack strategic issues throughout the company. These issues needed to be managed differently in each of the business areas of the company. The first emphasis was on hardware 10× improvement, followed by software 10× improvement, and halving their break-even time (BET) for generating profit on new product developments was the third. What HP did by creating these strategic focuses was to emphasize their product innovation process. If you improve your hardware and software quality and get your products out quicker—that's the basic formula for success. BET implies design quality—Young's whole system of strategic focus really implied design quality.

Therefore, Quantum Quality *is* innovation, implying the same dynamics: the development and implementation of both large leaps and small steps that produce new ways to do things differently or better. The large leaps can emerge from a series of incremental improvements all focused on one activity (which could lead to a short-term leap up), or they can represent a more complete break with the past.

Fred Schwettman's management team at HP took a quantum leap in commitment and effectiveness. They went beyond TQM's emphasis on empowerment, team accountability, customer–supplier focus, and speed. His comments, which follow, reveal the additional set of key success dimensions for Quantum Quality: learning, values, creativity, and sustainability.

Learning. *What was really fascinating to me was how hard it is to learn this. I'm on a planning and quality committee at HP. One of my peers said, "You've got to focus on results." So, I said, "Suppose I listened to your boss's presentations at our management counsel and he says, 'Look at this profitability and look at this great product; the results are spectacular.' I can listen to him talk about results from now 'til doomsday and that's not going to help me learn to manage my business better. If I were to say, 'Tell me about the process you use in arriving at decisions to get these good results' then all of a sudden, I've learned something really valuable."*

Values. *I attach a lot of importance to people understanding what it is they're trying to achieve out of work and how that relates to personal purpose. What can I contribute to people's lives? I also have to spend my time trying to figure out how we'll survive with results within this industry, which is horrible in terms of its competitiveness. But overall, it's like when the time comes to check out, you better feel really good about what you accomplished . . . and making a little profit here and there is probably not going to cut it.*

Creativity. *Creativity can be just as powerful in a structured approach as it can in a free-for-all, but it takes time. A lot of creativity goes into the processes. I think in the early stages, it probably took a little creativity away from the results side of it because people felt constrained. Once we got to the point where the process was understandable, we brought creativity to each part of it. People started to generate the good ideas and novel approaches. The people became really excited about it once they saw that it left you with your creativity.*

Sustainability. *What was most amazing about the team that led our new quality effort was how they said, "We're never going to get something good out of this by just going out and studying what other people have done. We've got to do an experiential thing where we change. They didn't sort of give it the intellectual approach of well, here's a good course, let's teach it. It was like, "Wow, that looks really interesting, let's take it and internalize it." What happened was very interesting. Anybody who would talk to these people would end up saying, "Boy, that's a different person than I remember." One thing we concluded was very important for the longevity of quality was: We never call it a quality* program *because people always associate programs with finite horizons; and it's never a* project *because people think they can go back to old ways of doing things when the project is over. It is either called the quality* process *or the quality* transformation.

Quality Transformation is another name for Quantum Quality. These four new dimensions of the Quantum Quality paradigm will be discussed in detail in the next chapter.

2

Working Smarter, Richer, Better, Healthier

We've grown substantially. The employee population that we're supporting has increased by 79 percent in the last five years. To keep head count flat, we've had to make some dramatic improvements.

> —Marie Clements, director of payroll and benefit administration, UNUM Life Insurance Company of America

For Marie Clements, making dramatic improvements has meant computerizing her departments as well as improving work processes in the areas she manages.

> *Three years ago, the payroll and benefits staff at UNUM had no PCs, no automatic spreadsheets or anything like that. The mainframe system handled some processing but everything else was done manually. We even still had grey metal boxes filled with cardex cards. So my challenge was to see if we could get people equipment, get them trained, teach them how to use it and then push them beyond. We needed to look at how people are doing work and make improvements. The business we want to be in is really adding value to this corporation and being the change agents by driving a lot of new initiatives.*

Payroll and benefits had to handle all the paper forms for updating personnel files, including timesheets, employee profiles (e.g., addresses), benefits changes, and more. The time needed to put these data into their computer systems was enormous.

> *For example, if I moved, I wouldn't be able to just directly change my address. I'd have to go to my manager to get my profile form and then fill it in with my new address; we would both sign it and send it on its way. All*

that my staff did was input that change once they received it—they added absolutely no value to that data, just typed it in. Then one of my people had to mail the updated form back to the manager once the computer generated it.

Marie realized that, to the extent that she had people inputting information that had already passed through several hands, they were losing an opportunity. Her challenge was to capture data at the source, by allowing the people who want to make the changes to make them directly, thereby eliminating her staff from the loop. Then, her related goal was to give her staff work that adds real value.

There were many systems and work processes Marie's group targeted for improvement . . . and not just incremental improvement. In studying the situation, the group found many different opportunities for improvement. For example, one of the early targets was the weekly timesheet system. Marie's group began to envision the system very differently.

In our company we have a very sophisticated population in terms of the personal computers (PCs) available to them. We were trying to leverage that and allow people to interact with us very differently.

For example, we imagined replacing the timesheet with a system where people could just call up a particular screen on their personal computer or their terminal, and it would have a timesheet all filled out for them? . . . If they have no changes all they have to do is push a button. It automatically goes to their manager's electronic in-box. The manager looks at it and pushes a button to approve it and send it along or reject it with a reason and send it back to the employee. It automatically generates transactions to the payroll system so we are out of that loop. Once we imagined it, we built it.

Salary, vacation, and tax information is now also available so employees can look at it whenever they want without calling Marie's staff.

Another aspect of making this a creative, breakthrough solution was getting the different computer systems to talk to one another.

We were able to build some bridges back and forth between systems. One allowed you, with only one ID and password, to go into all of the systems for which you were authorized. (Previously each had its own ID and password.) We had to work with other areas to make this happen, but it worked and everyone benefited.

In another example, if you're my manager and I submit a timesheet to you, a couple times a day the system would send a note to managers across that bridge into the electronic-mail that says, "This person has submitted a

timesheet for your approval; please go into the timesheet system. It's not per-
fect, but there're a lot of things going on behind the scenes that are pretty
invisible to the customer.

The implementation of the new system had many benefits.

We've put the information directly in the hands of the user. The basic princi-
ple is capture information at its source and give it to the people who need it.
So, we're trying to make sure that the people who want to make the changes
can make the changes themselves and then the people who need the informa-
tion have it. It gets us out of that loop, and our customers are much happier.

Marie and many others realize that such quantum improvements are
absolutely essential today, in response to the changing rules of the business game. Walter Kiechel III, assistant managing editor of *Fortune* magazine, said as much in his article, "The Organization That Learns":

As Corporate America edges nervously into the 1990s, it could really use a
new paradigm of the successful business organization. The old bureaucratic
command-and-control model, even in its current decentralized, lean-and-
mean version, won't be up to the challenges ahead: It won't be fast enough, it
won't be keen enough, it won't be smart or sensitive enough.[1]

To gain competitive advantage during the 1960s, a strong emphasis was
placed on technology development. The 1970s added an emphasis on cost
controls and quality assurance, employing the dimensions of inspection,
measurement of results, statistical analysis, and process improvement. In
the 1980s, the emphasis was placed on TQM and its dimensions of
employee empowerment, team accountability, customer focus, and speed
(including cycle-time reduction).

Today, these past emphases and dimensions are still necessary and
yet *insufficient* to gain and maintain leadership in business. The problem is
that so many companies are getting good at them that they're now the
basic requirements *to be in* the game and yet don't provide the creative,
competitive edge *to win* the game.

To gain a sustainable advantage in serving customers better than anyone else, QQ *includes but expands* on TQM with the newer dimensions of

- Learning
- Values

---

[1] "The Organization That Learns," *Fortune*, March 12, 1990, pp. 133–135.

- Creativity

- Sustainability

thereby producing breakthroughs in product, service, and process improvements that are better-targeted, more motivated, more creative, and more responsive. In other words, Quantum Quality is working *smarter, richer, better, healthier.*

Marie's story illustrates the dimensions of learning, values, creativity, and sustainability that contributed to the quantum quality breakthrough at UNUM Life Insurance Co.

LEARNING. Learning began with the needs analysis.

We're fortunate we have a lot of people with the right attitude here who want this kind of paperless world where our customers can really benefit. There is also a very high level of trust and collaboration between our systems staff and those of us on the business side. This was a critical success factor. We listened. We talked to customers ahead of time and found out what their concerns were and tried to address them. We tried to make sure that we hadn't missed any opportunity.

But learning had to go beyond that and be built into the new systems to make Marie's group as productivity-enhancing and cost-effective as possible.

With the old forms, there was no place to give anyone directions for using them. The information came to us incorrect, incomplete, and inaccurate, so we had to follow up—another inconvenience, and one that we were guilty of creating ourselves. So we put together a quality action team to figure out how to close this gap. They are now creating an on-line reference guide that will combine a philosophy statement with some real practical "here's what you need to do" info.

In going forward with these improvements, learning continues to be involved. This was challenging for Marie and her staff, as not everyone was happy with the progress they had made.

There seemed to be a gap in understanding about what we had accomplished. People wanted more, and wanted it faster. Part of working that through was sitting down with different heads of the areas and asking, "What is your perception of this organization, of what it has accomplished, and of where it's going?"—forcing myself to just listen to what they said and not question it, react to it, or defend. It was very powerful. It was also very painful, but it illuminated the gap in communication and education. It helped me see from their perspective. Now I know where they are and can try to improve the situation.

VALUES. What drives people like Marie and her staff to put forth the effort to make such improvements?

First of all I'm certainly not doing it alone. There are other people who have been just as instrumental. I don't know that there's any one of us that single-handedly created the vision.

Why do I continue to play the game? It's very rewarding. We can see that we're making a real impact, really improving how things are done here. That just feels good. It's not how much they pay me. It's just that personal satisfaction from knowing you've done a really good job. It makes it more fun. Wouldn't you rather come to work in the morning to a job that's fun and exciting rather than one that's boring and drudgery?

Yet it's not all peaches and cream, either. It takes character to stay with that struggle, to persevere until the next leap is made possible.

It's also empowering to stand back and to say what's going wrong here? Sometimes you have to live with it for awhile before you can fix it. It's not all rosy . . . and while we've accomplished an awful lot, it hasn't been without some struggle. I'm struggling with, "What do we do now? How do we stay on track? How can we maintain management commitment and get the resources we need to make the changes?"

CREATIVITY. Marie's team wanted to go beyond incremental improvements.

We asked, 'Where are the home runs . . . in making the kinds of major changes with how our customers interact with us?'

What helped them to find the breakthroughs?

It's having people that can think outside the boxes. You've got to have people that aren't willing to accept that it's impossible or it won't work. If you put people alone in a box, they're not nearly as creative as when you put them in a room with other people who have a lot of ideas. You can build on a kernel of a good idea. You explore the objections while you continue to push those barriers.

For example, we actually have two huge mainframe computers here. Our electronic mail system lives on one. The payroll system lives on the other one. Until this point those two could never talk to each other. There was no need to. What we wanted to do was to build some bridges between those systems even though some people said it couldn't be done. By assembling the right team we were able to get where we wanted to go.

SUSTAINABILITY. For long term sustainability, everyone must feel the benefit .

My hope is that the jobs in my area will change substantially as people stop inputting information where they add no value. What they will keep is a much better, more rewarding job, using critical thinking skills—the things that we can't automate. They also get to branch out and become trainers and mentors in how to use the system—rather than sitting there inputting all day.

The benefit has been not just to her area, but to the whole company.

It's easier for every employee to have that one ID and password, to get into all the systems and be able to jump around between systems. We're really looking at how can we give our customers, the employees, all the information they need at their fingertips, and make it as easy as possible for them. It's been an incredible tool for managers because they now have the information for all of the people who report to them available in one place.

We also saw in Fred Schwettman's story how these four dimensions were fundamental to improving the management leadership of quality at HP. They demonstrate that there's an *inner game and an outer game of quality* to be won. The *inner game* requires that we *learn* and put our personal *values* to work—to focus on and commit to finding creative solutions to quality problems. The *outer game* requires that we implement specific ways to be *creative* in a *sustainable* way. Winning with quality requires continuous development of both games. The payoff is greater satisfaction and better bottom line results.

Given the recession-prone and highly competitive environments of the 1990s, quality improvement is faced with three alternative paths:

- Using TQM in a "reactionary way" as the "packaging" for more authoritarian, command-and-control management[2]

---

[2] For example, management could become panicky if an economic recession doesn't turn around, or if people feel empowered enough to threaten the existing structures. The temptation could be to think, "Here's a way for us to exert management control." This temptation is exacerbated today when management wants to emulate those companies who have been more successful by applying quality improvement, yet without embracing the key dimensions of QQ.

- Practicing TQM's traditional dimensions of empowerment, teamwork, and so on, with its emphasis on incremental improvements
- Employing the four new dimensions of Quantum Quality: learning, values, creativity, and sustainability.

It might still seem that the four dimensions of learning, values, creativity, and sustainability, by themselves, don't indicate a paradigm shift in thinking about the quality game. Let's examine the expansive shift that's being evoked in each of these areas, and its impact, this time using R&D as an example.

Learning

Early in 1987, Frank Carrubba was named director of Hewlett-Packard Laboratories (HPL), an organization whose "business" is creativity, innovation, and quality improvement. Frank noted that if his teams were 100 percent successful in everything they tried—"zero defects R&D"—then he'd know they were setting safe goals and not stretching the edges of what's possible. Yet, testing those edges was essential to keep HP in the position of technological leadership, of fastest market response, and of highest quality (by design).

So Frank began to think about how to reward "intelligent failure," where valuable learning occurred on troubled projects that could still benefit future projects. In a sense, he was expanding the types of answers to the question, "How can we make sure we're successful?"

> If a failure is "intelligent", it's just as good as—if not better than—success because it teaches you what not to do. And it teaches you how to understand what you've done so that you can apply it in a new and different way if the opportunity comes in the future. What's needed is the trust that you build in your teams and support for accepting that.

This is just one aspect of the Quantum Quality dimension of learning. TQM has always celebrated learning from customers and the process of defining their expectations. Technologies, competitive climate, employee values—all these are changing so fast. How do we keep up? How do we avoid information overload? How do we stay competent enough to ensure that we respond well? How do we turn a collection of individual learners into an intelligent learning community?

A great deal of attention is being put into the importance and development of the "learning organization." The more complete and accurate term is the "innovative learning organization." The two words belong together in the same breath, because in fact they are the twin complements needed for business health and prosperity: You might say that learning is the inhaling, and innovative improvement is the exhaling. Peter Senge, author of *The Fifth Discipline*, says, "In contemporary speech, the meaning of learning has been dragged down to 'taking in information.' We should think of learning as the expansion of one's capacity to create, to produce results."[3] *Learning* expands one's creative capacity. *Innovation* is the creative usage of that expanded capacity.

This inhaling–exhaling process must be done *continuously* under the rapidly changing set of business conditions today. Again, here is Walter Kiechel III of *Fortune* magazine:

> *A learning organization takes the idea of continuous improvement seriously. One question is never very far from the thoughts of its people: "How can this be done better?" Learning includes letting them try out the new and occasionally make the most awful mistakes. Particularly astute companies will realize that different people learn, and improve matters, in different ways.*[4] *(emphasis mine)*

Practical knowledge of those "different ways" is just one part of what this book offers.

Values

At the Baldrige Award ceremony honoring Federal Express as the first service company to win the award, Fred Smith, founder and CEO, said "In trying to understand the service side of quality, one must necessarily grasp the significance of the human side of quality." Rosabeth Moss Kanter, formerly of the *Harvard Business Review*, adds,

> *"Now we're putting much more responsibility in the hands of workers to correct problems themselves because that saves time, that's a better guarantee of quality, . . . After all, business strategy can be articulated at the top of the*

---

[3] Peter Senge, *The Fifth Discipline: Mastering the Five Practices of the Learning Organization* (New York: Doubleday, 1990).

[4] Kiechel, op. cit.

firm, but what it really means in practice is what the ordinary worker does, because that's often what the customer sees."[5]

When Frank Carrubba took over HP Labs in 1987, he conducted a study of what were the most significant differences between teams that failed to achieve their objectives, teams that were successful, and teams that produced extraordinary results well beyond their own or others' expectations. After comparing the findings for the consistently superior teams with the marginally successful teams, Frank noted that the teams were equal in terms of talent, motivation, and the ability to create realistic goals. As to the difference:

If you look at those (superior) teams that were truly successful, we found that those teams had leaders and managers, sometimes the same person and sometimes not, who found in themselves qualities of spirit and truth, and they brought it out in their customers.

Those teams that really stood out treated their customers as they themselves wanted to be treated. They had a relationship with their customers that was a personal relationship, one that allowed people to be all that they could be and not worry about struggling day after day trying to represent themselves as being something that they weren't.

These teams were made up of researchers, then, who saw the people in other Hewlett-Packard divisions as customers! And they *found in themselves qualities of spirit and truth*—important values of interpersonal support and personal integrity.

The bottom line of this story is amazing: In a high-tech industry, with rapid product development times, talent and motivation and vision could carry a team only just so far. To fully optimize and expand those resources, personal values such as caring for their (internal and external) customers and communicating with integrity and authenticity made the significant difference between "plain" success and extraordinary results.

With Quantum Quality, these fundamental human values become part and parcel of raising the levels of breakthroughs in process improvement, customer delight, and personal commitment. It's even more than simply aligning personal and organizational values, as TQM has often done so effectively. It's exploring the notion that fundamental human values—truth, inner peace, right conduct, and love, and concern for the well-

---

[5] Quoted in Lloyd Dobyns and Clare Crawford-Mason, *Quality or Else* (Boston: Houghton-Mifflin, 1991), p. 115.

being of others—are intrinsic to supporting established business values such as quality, creativity, communication, excellence, and service.

These human values are found in all the world's great religions. Therefore, contrary to the skeptical view of many in the business community, ethical, spiritual considerations can be intrinsic to running a successful business.[6]

Creativity

Originated in manufacturing environments, TQM has played out themes such as "conformance to high standards," "reduced variation," "zero defects," "doing the right thing," and "doing things right the first time."

People in marketing and R&D have often resisted quality programs that emphasize "doing things right the first time." They believe that failures are an integral part of the process of testing new customer responses or new experimental designs. When people are under the pressure to "do it right the first time," it often halts the experimentation and creative thinking for trying to improve work processes. The notion of "zero defects" is hard to apply, and it has often led to finger pointing and fault-finding when this impossible ideal is never reached. [7]

This is one reason why quality-improvement programs often have a very difficult time being accepted and implemented in functions such as R&D and marketing, where having the room to think creatively is recognized as essential to doing the work. Yet, even strategy development can be a creative exercise under Quantum Quality—developing insights into our business and markets, generating a wide variety of strategic options from which to choose, flushing out the best alternatives, and ensuring that plans are not only formulated but carried out.

As Frank Carrubba said,

Creativity comes from within. I think what differentiates a good project is (1) that it works and what comes out at the end is state of the art, and (2) that it's

---

[6] I don't expect that people will automatically believe this at first reading. However, it is an element of "new paradigm thinking" with regards to Quantum Quality.

[7] Such negative consequences were never part of the intentions or theories of the original leaders of the quality movement. They've simply become part of the historical reality of implementing quality improvement in the United States and many other countries.

an adventure and an exciting time for the people involved in doing it. So this opportunity allows me to create an environment where we are always striving to be better and to create an environment where people know that the name of the game is to be all that you can be.

Carrubba's first issue when he took over at Hewlett-Packard Labs was setting a new direction for the creative talent he found there. The group's creativity had to be focused on designing in high quality from the outset and truly serving emerging customer needs.

Once you start becoming complacent is when you end up in trouble. The world is moving rapidly, and you start drifting into the future with something that appears in your rear-view mirror, so to speak. We have to ensure that we don't do that.

When I was asked to become the director of HP Labs, it could not continue being what it was in the past. . . . What I clearly saw was that the customers were looking for systems-oriented solutions that in most cases required multidisciplinary contributions, which required synergism above and beyond anything we had seen here in the past.

The HP company wanted something they could depend on but also something that would really create leadership products. It required stepping away from that comfortable autonomous kind of environment to one where you had to give and take, push and shove, give and receive from your colleagues.

Often, creative leadership and thinking skills are missing from TQM programs. Most TQM tools emphasize analysis and focusing on the right issues. Then, and only then, comes the creative process of generating the potential "quality improvements" themselves. And *quality improvement*, after all, is the application of *creativity* to solving problems in *work processes* ($Q_i = C \times W_p$), to produce both breakthroughs and incremental change.

For example, one client has a 3-inch-thick manual for training quality team leaders on the TQM tools. Only after working through about 2 inches of the manual does a person complete his or her analysis of the quality problems and priorities. There's only one page devoted to actually generating an improvement per se: "brainstorm possible solutions." Apparently, the assumption is that if your analysis is sufficient, the improvement should be obvious—or that a "miracle" may happen.

Therefore, to develop leadership not only in products but also in processes, one very prominent contribution to quality improvement that the dimension of creativity can add is in generating real *improvements*.

Some organizations such as DuPont are even beginning to apply the term "continuous improvement" to denote the development of both incremental and breakthrough improvements. DuPont's Center for Creativity and Innovation has a logo in which the letters "CI" stand for "Creativity/Innovation" *and* "Continuous Improvement." Thus, as we have seen, "continuous improvement" is premised on continuous learning.

Sustainability

There's one other key dimension that is integral to Quantum Quality: that of *sustainability*. Much in the ways that we work—as individuals, businesses, and nation states—is simply not conducive to long-term growth and vitality. As individuals, eight out of ten of us in the United States end up dying from so-called lifestyle illnesses, such as cancer and high blood pressure. (A century ago, the main causes were viral or natural aging.) As businesses, we have long bowed to quarterly profit pressures from Wall Street, at the expense of longer-term investment for positioning our companies for growth and change. As nation states, we have operated according to laws that often sacrifice the environment for economic growth, at great future expense for cleanup and health.

Just as health means *wellness*, not just "not sick," sustainable means *thriving*, not just "surviving." Having a sustainable advantage means going beyond the normal understanding of competitive advantage.

Sustainable development means making the present system (such as business and nation) progress in such way as to avoid damaging—and even *enhance*—our long-term prospects. Sustainability requires a true community consciousness, mandating that we go beyond self-interest and instead value and take responsibility for the whole. TQM has fostered strong relationship with a business' suppliers and customers; QQ implies breaking down the walls between, not only customers or suppliers, but competitors as well.

Having a *sustainable advantage* in one's business means "serving customers better than anyone else," not "beating the competition." Although these may sound similar, the latter determines customer needs through the filter of a competitor's success; the former learns of customer needs directly, with a greater probability of being able to capitalize on that relationship.

This may well be the most radical part of Quantum Quality. And the question remains, "What does it mean to work and profit in a sustainable way for long-term growth and vitality?"

One night over dinner, Frank Carrubba asked what I thought was the part of his job, as worldwide R&D director of HP Labs, that took more of his time than anything else. "Meetings?" I asked. But his answer was, "Deciding what NOT to do." There were so many opportunities to act that it was critical not to waste time on any that lay in the way of the critical path of success for the company as a whole.[8]

So, to achieve this level of speed in R&D, Frank had to develop a strong sense of common understanding throughout HP Labs—not only of the mission and vision, but also of the business environment and the key success factors that made the researchers' work critical.

> *The only way you're going to achieve this is with a team of managers that are equally inspired and motivated to fulfill the same goals. We proceeded in developing an answer to this single question that I asked them: "Why are we here at HP Labs and what difference do we make in this company?" And the followup, "Why are you here within HP Labs and what difference do you make?" "Why we're here?" means "What do we want to be? What is it that we want to be for the HP Company?" "What you want to be" is your purpose in life.*

Without this emphasis, time and effort would be wasted heading in unnecessary directions that would not serve the long-term sustainability of HP's business—and being cautious about taking the risks necessary to achieve quantum results.

As noted earlier, the *inner game* of QQ requires that we *learn* and put our personal *values* to work—to focus on and commit to finding creative solutions to quality problems. The *outer game* requires that we practice specific means to be *creative* in a *sustainable* way.

The Quantum Quality dimensions of learning, values, creativity, and sustainability, can enhance very specific quality improvement projects, not just the management of large functions like R&D. Take, for example, the project work led by Cynthia Gaudette, a project manager in the retirement security area at UNUM Life Insurance Company of America. She works with groups of system analysts and business people who have a background of processing in a service or accounting area to figure out why something's a problem, how we can fix it, what it would cost, what's

---

[8] Even though Frank was also tolerant of intelligent failure, he wanted at least to be aimed in the right direction.

the benefit—and then making recommendations to management. One specific project involved the reconciliation of three different computer systems run in the retirement security area.

They had been entering similar data in all three systems and then reconciling the three systems to make sure they matched.

> *We spent time and money to hire people to enter it three times; and then we spent the time and money to hire people to reconcile it after we entered it. Then we couldn't deliver statements to our customers until we knew that all three systems balanced.*

In 1990, management introduced a quality program called Operating Excellence and a new vice president noted the millions of dollars spent doing this reconciliation process. A subsequent quality action team asked, "Why don't we just input the information *once* and then have the other systems read it to everywhere that it needs to go?" By paying somebody only once to enter data and bypassing the need to reconcile, they would be able to send out statements sooner. The cost-benefit analysis showed a significant improvement for customer service and a potential savings.

> *Phase 1 ended up being just incredible. Usually you never decrease resources on the day you implement. But everything had been done so well. On the day we implemented we decreased from 12 people down to 6. Even at that we could have still reduced more. We used the other 6 people on other projects. That was a big success story, benefits even from Phase 1.*
>
> *When we get to Phase 3, we should have another quantum leap. One system will be feeding all the others, so there shouldn't be much of an effort to do reconciliation. We should see significant reduction in staff at the same time we see speed to the customer improved.*

Cynthia's comments about their success show the role of the Quantum Quality dimensions.

LEARNING. They spent time learning about each other's work priorities, their customers, and how to share their results.

> *The first thing you have to do is get everyone up to speed to understand what it is everyone else does and why they do it. We had some problems. We found out even more of just how important it is, upfront, to let people get to know each other, establish a mission, establish roles and responsibilities, and determine how you are going to make decisions. Luckily, we caught it in time—so we were able to pull it through.*

VALUES. They worked to fulfill intrinsic motivations, not financial rewards.

Sometimes I think about the frustrations and ask, "Why do I do this?" I know how great it will be for the people who work here. There is frustration over this whole reconciliation process, and people have to work so hard. What drives me and others on this project is that we just can't wait to be able to give people something that's going to make their lives so much easier. It's the right thing to do, so we want to do it.

CREATIVITY. They aimed beyond incremental improvement on the existing system.

I think that's what made the big breakthroughs possible in this—because we had this new process. Operating Excellence, where we learned how to go deeper to find out what the real problem is. . . . People are usually looking for the quick fix—looking at problems and trying to put band aids on them. For years, the word "reconciliation" meant problems, but instead of trying to figure out why we even reconciled in the first place, we'd just look at how to make the process easier.

SUSTAINABILITY. They aimed for the long term solution, getting involvement and buy-in to the issue from every key party.

One of the things our project is doing is getting our three major areas working together on the same project to make sure that we give everyone what they need. Naturally, working with three groups, dynamic tension occasionally occurs. We view these as opportunities to better learn about the objectives and processes of one another's work, and then together we work toward understanding, which creates broad-based buy-in.

One thing that helps is that we have a Steering Committee with the heads of each of the three areas. Once a month we bring to them any issues that we have and they give us perspective and direction on how to proceed.

Every one of us, and every one of our companies, has a stake in how well we produce high-quality goods and services that continually meet the changing needs of the market. But beyond making money, there's our basic need for personal growth and meaningful success in our work. Personal growth is based on continuous learning. Meaningful success comes through continuous improvement, not resting on yesterday's achievements.

Quantum Quality does not replace what has already been accomplished in fostering better quality in the workplace (e.g., the work of

Deming, Juran, and Crosby); it adds important new elements to "expand" the statistical and incremental nature of many TQM programs. The field of creativity also offers a great deal to this enhancement, along with the emerging notion of the "learning organization." In this new synthesis, you will find ways to draw upon and apply learning, values, creativity, and sustainability to find quantum leaps in process improvement, customer delight and personal/team commitment.

The general goal remains the same: to find ways to be the best we can be in the coming decades.

3

Success Is a Journey,
Not a Destination

A couple of years ago, we went through a reduction in force which in and of itself was emotionally devastating to the entire office. A normal reduction in force consists of taking people out who are your sub-standard performers.

What I did was I took a blank sheet of paper and I said to myself so what is it that you want your organization to do. I literally started from scratch and built the entire organization structure, which was very different from the existing organization structure. Needless to say, it caused some grief.

—Linda Smith, former vice president, Heller
Financial Corporation, Leveraged Financial Group

Corporate clients come to Heller's LFG to obtain financing for any number of reasons: to buy a company, to grow, to pay out their current lender, and so on. As Linda describes it,

It gets into a pretty intricate analysis. We want to know as much about that company if not more than the owners do, so we take a very business-oriented approach to how we lend rather than just looking strictly at assets or some other collateral. We either take a warrant or an option or a capital appreciation right or some equity instrument, so we're interested in two things: we're interested in our return of principal and we're interested in return of equity. Therefore, our interest is in making that business as successful as possible.

How Linda dealt with downsizing the organization is the feature story of this chapter.

Quality improvement is more than just fixing problems. Improving quality at Hewlett-Packard Labs, or any successful business, is essentially like taking a journey—a whole process that encompasses everything from defining a clear goal or destination, focusing on the key issues, finding a creative solution, and completing the implementation and measurement of success.

The Quantum Quality process, then, is a creative journey that has four main stages:

1. *Set a Destination:* ***The Challenge.*** Determine your goal and confront the uncertainty of achieving it.
2. *Choose a Vehicle:* ***The Focus.*** Realize your power to succeed and define the elements of your challenge more clearly.
3. *Travel:* ***The Creative Solutions.*** Develop creative options and decide on the most valuable solution to you.
4. *Arrive:* ***The Completion.*** Implement your solution and find satisfaction in your learning and achievements along the way.

As seen in Figure 3.1, the Creative Journey™ is actually a cyclical process. For quality improvement in particular, this is truly a "Creative Journey," because it entails not just analyzing quality problems, but applying creativity to develop the best possible improvement. By getting to know the stages of the journey, we can greatly increase our chances of producing creative insights and putting those insights to work effectively.

Linda Smith managed her challenge according to this Creative Journey process.

The Challenge

I have relationships with every single person in this office. I went through a lot of inner turmoil, as you can imagine. The finance group has been contracting and centralizing over the years. And what that has meant is layoffs at the division level. I tried to take a leap forward and say if they determine that this should be totally centralized, "How is it that I want my finance function to operate and what is it I really want from them?" "How can I do this downsizing and still maintain everyone's dignity?"

The Focus

We had sixty people in this office. With our clients, we have to structure a financial package that services both their needs as well as ours. When we look at a transaction we have a marketing department who does at least [an] initial pass at structuring it. Then we have an underwriting department that gets into the real detail of industry analysis and management analysis.

4. THE
COMPLETION

1. THE
CHALLENGE

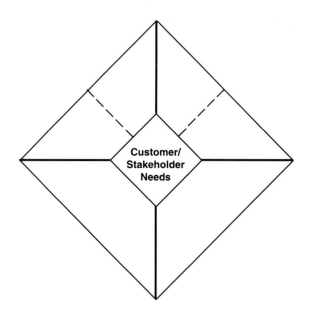

3. THE
CREATIVE
SOLUTIONS

2. THE
FOCUS

FIGURE 3.1.   The Creative Journey™

I asked, "What is it I want of each function?" I went through and ratio-nalized every single position. When it comes to reducing the numbers of jobs I really do take this stuff to heart and I don't like letting people go. So what I try to do is say what skills does that person have that might fit somewhere else in the organization. If not here, then where. I try to do it through attri-tion so that I'm not in a continual state of reduction of staff.

It took a great deal of time and effort on my part. There are those who would say that I should have done that in a team environment. I didn't for morale reasons. I didn't think it was appropriate to have everybody else as upset as I was.

The Creative Solutions
I took my audit unit and my finance department and combined those units. I removed levels of management to the extent necessary. I pushed that work down to lower levels so that they were empowered with a greater sense of

responsibility and authority. And we just totally wiped out the clerical func-tion. We have established a local area network within the office which reduced the need for secretaries.

Everybody said there's no way that that ever works. No way. People in headquarters said it. People here said it. My own management team was dubious.

Of those 25 people laid off, 15 of them were in functions that we didn't need anymore. The remaining 10 were people who no longer had the skill base I needed. So in some of these cases I might have had a person who's perform-ing very well in a previous job but I still had to lay them off.

I fought and fought for the absolutely best severance packages I could give these people and I fought for doing the entire act in a way that they could keep their dignity about them.

The Completion

We had the management team spend a Sunday off site organizing the announcement day. We had an outplacement group already set up so that after we talked to the people individually we could send them directly to the outplacement company.

We said, look, we are going to help you. We have outplacement. We're going to help you find jobs. We're going to pay you for this long a period of time and we feel very very badly about this. But from a business perspective we don't have a choice. The way I came around was I guess doing the best I could for them. It still killed me. It was all I could do.

I have had people tell me that when I've fired them they didn't feel like they've been fired; that it was handled so nicely that they didn't feel really bad about it. They could go on to the next level of their lives. Probably half of the people who were let go came in and said goodbye to me and they under-stood. I got a few hugs and with that kind of support I was able to make it through. I'm very lucky I have very wonderful people I work with. I mean that sincerely.

After we announced the reduction in force, I said to the remaining staff, "You have to make this work. I challenge you to go out and look at what you're doing . . . and if you don't need to do it and you can't figure out a rea-son why you've been doing it except that it's been done for years, quit it." They asked, "Do we have to get your approval?" And I said, "I do not have to approve; I trust you to be able to rationalize your functions." Now we're talk-ing down to secretaries here. "If you are just filling out a stupid piece of paper—quit. Chances are nobody's going to miss it. And nobody did."

This was two years ago October that we did this. A year ago we had Coopers & Lybrand audit all the company offices and our office was touted without question as being the most efficient, the best organized, the best communicators, and the most knowledgeable about their businesses.

The bottom line is hard to measure in our business first of all. Our portfolio is still about $400 million. My expenses were 50% compensation and about 50% G&A; I now have 75% comp and 25% G&A. I had $3 million in G&A. I've now got about $900,000. The interesting part of that is that it has been a continually improving number. It has not stopped yet. The number just keeps going down. So what's happened is that between the compensation reductions and G&A reductions, our bottom line is up about $3 million.

Quantum Quality and the Creative Journey

To be more specific about the Quantum Quality process, each stage of this Creative Journey has two steps (see Figure 3.2):

1. The Challenge:
   - Establish a goal.
   - Meet and confront the uncertainty of achieving it.
2. The Focus:
   - Tap into your character: realize your power to succeed.
   - Analyze issues: define the elements of your challenge more clearly.
3. The Creative Solutions:
   - Generate creative options.
   - Decide on the most valuable solution.
4. The Completion:
   - Implement your solution.
   - Celebrate the results—your learning and improvements.

Many of those reading this may practice the Shewhart cycle for quality improvement: Plan–Do–Check–Act. The word Plan has a lot of work implied in it, taking up the first three stages of the Creative Journey: Challenge, Focus, and Creative Solutions. Do–Check happens at the borders of the "Creative Solutions" stage and the Completion stage: The doing and checking are part of the experimentation with possible solutions until one is chosen. Then, Act takes place primarily in the Completion stage, implementing the solution thoroughly.

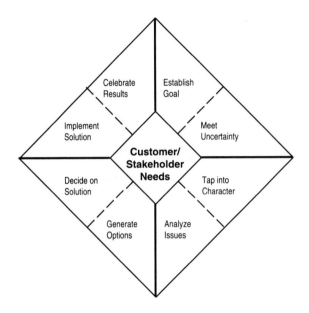

4. THE
COMPLETION

1. THE
CHALLENGE

3. THE
CREATIVE
SOLUTIONS

2. THE
FOCUS

FIGURE 3.2. The Creative Journey™

Whether the challenge is for R&D, marketing, or manufacturing, the following more detailed description of the Creative Journey's stages and steps can apply.

In the *Challenge* stage, you'll discover your general sense of purpose and begin to meet with any barriers to fulfilling that purpose. This is the point where you may find yourself to be "in a mess" as you're facing the uncertainties of a new situation.

As a quick look at how this process works in real life, consider the case of Joe Workland, plant manager at PW Pipe in Portland, Oregon. He began his QQ process facing the challenge of needing to speed up the changeovers from one pipe size to another on their pipe-making machines.

We took a look at our quick changeovers, something that over a year ago took us forty-five minutes to an hour. And when we took that concept that we can do these changeovers quicker to the plant personnel, they said, "No way. We been doing 'em this way; we do these every day; we're doing 'em as good as we can."

So we had to develop a tool that would allow us to look at ourselves, to see how we were doing them and say, "We're not doing them wrong at this point, but we may have some opportunity to be able to do them faster, safer, and a little easier."

The *Focus* stage includes (1) applying skills of openness and flexibility and (2) gathering data and starting to tackle real problems. Here, you'll come to feel more self-confident in the midst of the uncertainty that lies ahead, and you'll be able to define the elements of your challenge more clearly.

To help Joe Workland focus on his challenge of improving plant efficiency, he borrowed an idea from one of the plant workers. The worker had seen a videotape on television comparing the speed of pit crews during Indy-500 pit stops. Joe decided to use a video camera to help him find the data that would allow him to focus on the real problem.

The video camera just has worked great for us. We videotaped our first changeover. And it was like putting eyes in the back of your head. The things that you're doing when you're on the line during that changeover are habitual: "This is the way we've always done it." Before this, we really haven't looked at new ways, nor has the company asked us for new ways or faster ways of accomplishing this changeover.'

By doing his homework, Joe made a new and creative solution possible.

The *Creative Solutions* stage is where you'll generate creative options and ideas and find a solution that's consistent with your values. During this stage, draw upon what you've discovered in the previous stages, the Challenge and the Focus, to inspire you.

Here's how Joe Workland put this idea to work at PW Pipe, generating as many options as he could to find the right solution to his creative challenge.

We sat in a room and said, "Let's look at this. Let's look at this videotape." You know. We did it in the morning. "Let's sit down and see how we did." And our approach was, "Here's the way we're doing our changeovers. There's nothing wrong with the way we're doing them, but is that the right way we should be doing them? Can we be doing them quicker? Can we make this look like a pit stop at the Indianapolis 500 race?" And from there, the ideas just mushroomed.

By getting the big picture, doing their homework, and being open and flexible, Joe Workland was able to find thoughtful solutions to their creative challenges.

For the *Completion* stage, it's appropriate to remind ourselves of the saying that creativity is 10 percent inspiration and 90 percent perspiration. And here's where the perspiration really comes in. In this stage, you'll implement your solution and then celebrate your results. Joe Workland is persistent, and he's looking forward to continuing success in his creative journey. But he hasn't forgotten to reward his co-workers and himself with recognition and a sense of pride in their achievement:

> *I get real excited when I look at that videotape of that last changeover. A year ago it was 45 minutes or an hour, and now we know we're down to five or six minutes. We know we can get it to three or four. Hopefully a year from now, maybe we're down to two! It's a continual improvement process. It's never over.*
>
> *From a recognition standpoint, we've had visits by three other plants saying, "How are you doing these changeovers? What's going on with this employee involvement?" And it's no longer the dummy plant manager taking the visitors on a plant tour. It's those guys out on the floor that know it all. Now it's them giving plant tours. And I think that's terrific.*

As busy as we all get sometimes, we often forget or neglect to celebrate what we've learned and what we've achieved. Yet, if you don't—if you just say, "Well that's that. All in a day's work. Gotta keep on keepin' on. What's next?"—it's likely that you'll burn out.

These celebrations don't have to be really big deals. Take even the simple pause that refreshes. It's also important to take time to acknowledge the feelings associated with not achieving something, or leaving that stimulating project or group behind, or ending a phase of your career. And be sure to include not only any feelings of sadness and regret, but also any feelings of gratitude as well.

There may be a period of rest and reflection as part of this stage. But a creative journey doesn't end there. The real completion only comes when you take what you've learned and achieved and bring it into your next challenge, to support the discovery of a new, renewed sense of purpose.

Joe Workland also found a new challenge—to pursue and develop the new ways of working that had helped him and his boss find the creative solutions they needed.

In a little over a year, there has been a dramatic turnaround in the quality of our operators and the way that our employee workforce is involved on the job. Traditionally, we said, "We want you to do this, and do it this way." Now we're asking them to be creative. And so we open up a whole new can of worms from, say, a management point of view, because sometimes it's pretty scary what these guys ask. But it's really exciting to hear they're really thinking about what they're working on.

Eight Steps to Empowering Quality Efforts

As we have seen, a new creative journey has begun arising from a greater sense of how effective you can be in putting your talents, your values, and your creative potential to work.

What does it mean to try to generate this creative quality improvement in today's workplace? In 1985, AT&T sponsored a study of the root implications of the word "quality" in the American culture, enlisting the help of Dr. Gilbert Rapaille. In the now-famous study,[1] they discovered that, in the U.S., the first experience of quality is usually negative, because it implies not producing what others wanted. "'Do it right the first time' was likely to demotivate rather than inspire higher performance."

Further, the study finds that for Americans quality resonates positively when associated with breakthrough, challenge, and new possibilities, but it resonates negatively when associated with standards, specifications, and control. (ibid., p. 11)

Furthermore, "The transformation process—which becomes the model for quality improvement—depends for its success on certain key roles" (ibid., p. 12). These roles are the Lawgiver, who communicates a crisis; the Mentor, who provides encouragement; the Coach, who supports movement toward breakthrough success; and the Celebrator, who recognizes the journey and achievements of the participants.

These roles fit perfectly into the four stages of the Creative Journey: the Lawgiver for the Challenge stage; the Mentor for the Focus stage; the Coach for the Creative Solutions stage; and the Celebrator for the Completion stage. The roles for stimulating the Quantum Quality process are thus very clear.

---

[1] see *Pathways*, ASQC, Milwaukee, WI, 1989.

For most Americans, quality should be a journey of exploration—a sense of upward and outward to explore where "no one has ever gone before." This is a journey that starts on the proven path of technical quality, but sooner or later encounters apathy, resistance, obstacles, or barriers. Along with that we must confront our defectiveness, sloppiness, or mess. We discover that the journey has rites of passage.

These moments of truth can cause us to look deeply within ourselves to draw upon resources. The deficiencies uncovered as we go bring us face to face with our deepest feelings of self worth. Quality expands to become human and emotional as well as technical. We experience a sense of growth, as quality includes the intuitive, sensitive, and caring elements as well as the intellectual, rational, logical forms. (ibid., p. 13)

Quality is using our creativity, imagination, and inventiveness to form a profound human connection between customers and employees (ibid., p. 14)

As shown in Figure 3.3, the next eight chapters provide eight practical means for you to attain a sustainable advantage in your work along each step of your Creative Journey. Each chapter will give you *principles and advice* on how to go through each step in a way that embodies the learning, values, creativity, and sustainability that Quantum Quality depends on.

Quantum Quality provides eight concrete ways, or principles, to accelerate and enhance the quality improvement work already going on in most companies:

1. Set goals beyond self-interest
2. Manage uncertainty rather than minimize risk
3. Make staff development a two-way street
4. Analyze issues from a "systems" perspective
5. Use four distinct strategies to find creative options
6. Reach speedy decisions based on group values
7. Assume leadership and managership at all levels
8. Reward focused learning as well as improvements

Each principle contributes to the mind-set that will help readers to incorporate learning, values, creativity, and sustainability. And by the end of the book, they'll also understand a unique framework for implementing the eight principles; chapter 7 describes how to strengthen "systems integrity" in the organizational culture while promoting personal growth, for the bot-

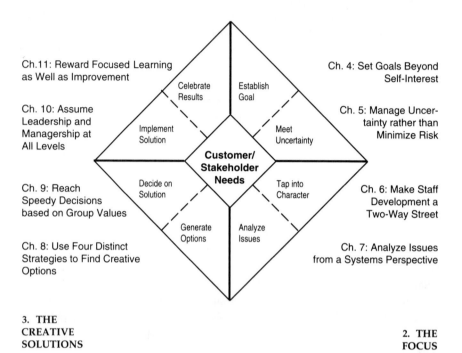

**4. THE
COMPLETION**

**1. THE
CHALLENGE**

Ch.11: Reward Focused Learning
as Well as Improvement

Celebrate
Results

Establish
Goal

Ch. 4: Set Goals Beyond
Self-Interest

Ch. 10: Assume
Leadership and
Managership at
All Levels

Implement
Solution

Meet
Uncertainty

Ch. 5: Manage Uncer-
tainty rather than
Minimize Risk

**Customer/
Stakeholder
Needs**

Ch. 9: Reach
Speedy Decisions
based on Group Values

Decide on
Solution

Tap into
Character

Ch. 6: Make Staff
Development a
Two-Way Street

Generate
Options

Analyze
Issues

Ch. 8: Use Four Distinct
Strategies to Find Creative
Options

Ch. 7: Analyze Issues
from a Systems Perspective

**3. THE
CREATIVE
SOLUTIONS**

**2. THE
FOCUS**

FIGURE 3.3.   The Creative Journey™

tom-line achievements and personal satisfaction that motivate continuous learning and improvement.

Again, each of the next eight chapters (comprising Part II) has three sections:

- *Mastering the Mind-Set*—explaining one of the eight QQ principles, with a significant success story illustrating how the principle is essential for breakthrough levels of quality improvement.

- *Strengthening the System*—explaining how you can incorporate each principle into workplace organizational systems to help "institutionalize" a culture of quality improvement.

- *Practicing the Paradigm*—showing how a principle can embody the four dimensions of learning, values, creativity, and sustainability in practical day-to-day work.

The first two sections/topics will apply most strongly to individuals and teams who are faced with Quantum Quality challenges in their work.

The third topic/section is very important for managers—and can be tricky! As mentioned earlier, "empowerment" has been one of the key values of TQM, along with customer focus and teamwork. Empowerment goes well beyond promoting a "can do" attitude. It even goes beyond teams having sufficient authority to solve quality challenges.

To be fully empowered, even a "high-performance team" (with vision, talent, and collaboration) needs strong alignment and linkage with its organizational culture. It requires that we manage the interface between work teams and their sponsoring management—those in charge of creating the "culture" of Quantum Quality—to give teams the greatest chance of succeeding throughout their Creative Journeys.

Based on a synthesis of research conducted at many corporations, universities, and nonprofit institutions—including Hewlett-Packard, the State University of New York at Buffalo, and the Stanford Research Institute—there seem to me to be sixteen key "make or break" factors that must be managed well for the organizational system to fully optimize a Quantum Quality culture. These factors are as follows:

A. Purpose/Vision

B. Roles/Authority

C. Business/Technology environment

D. Key success factors

E. Group values

F. Talent base

G. Communication structure

H. Information management

I. Team building/Idea support

J. Idea-generation strategies

K. Criteria

L. Decision-making process

M. Resource allocation

N. Transition management

O. Impact appraisal

P. Satisfaction/Rewards

These sixteen factors hold the key to establishing the management practices needed to build a Baldrige Award– or Deming Prize–winning culture. They also have a significant relationship to the eight steps in the Creative Journey. So, to give a "hands-on" practicality to the sometimes nebulous issue of managing the culture for Quantum Quality, each of the following eight chapters also gives concrete advice on managing two factors that will help you implement and "institutionalize" the QQ principles.

With the trend to cross-functional work groups and self-directed teams, creating the proper linkage between teams and sponsors is absolutely essential. This linkage can be even more difficult to develop if an organization is in the midst of a culture change—through downsizing, for example—or shifting from a more authoritarian to a more participative management style. The "hands-off" style of control and authority can be quite awkward.

Ultimately, our success with Quantum Quality depends in very large measure on how well we—as managers, team leaders, or team members—implement the dimensions, mind-sets, and management practices with complete personal *integrity*.

The word "integrity" stems from the same root as the words "integer" and "integral." The root means "oneness." Personal integrity thus means the "oneness"—the alignment, congruence, etc.—of what we believe, what we say, and what we actually do to back up our beliefs and words. The current expression is that we must "walk our talk." We must back up our visions and missions with concrete action. We must put our money where our mouths are.

At the level of thought and behavior, this leads naturally to ethical action. Using integrity, we're not caught in situations where we have to rationalize or excuse (to ourselves or to others) the fact that our actions don't really line up with our beliefs. And we're not caught trying to justify how we can direct others to follow something while not following it ourselves.

And beyond ethical behavior, integrity is essential to a quality-improvement program that depends on empowering people to find solutions to the problems they directly control in their jobs—one of the key contributions of TQM. Without integrity, there can be no trust. And without trust, there can be no power to empowerment.

To return to our original example for this chapter, for each of the four stages of the journey toward Quantum Quality, Linda Smith of Heller Financial Corp. discovered in herself some of the ways of creating a climate of empowerment in her division.

The Challenge

I've always believed that if you manage to the numbers you are not going to accomplish anything else other than maybe hitting the numbers. So each year we develop a word for the year. Last year our word was CREDIBILITY. Each letter stands for something. . . . The C was for Communications which are concise and consistent. R was for Recognition of employee performance. D was for Delivering what you promise—just basic management principals to aim for, centered on credibility.

The Focus

We have monthly office meetings. Everybody is tied to a bonus program, which is tied to the performance of the office. We review the office's monthly financial statement and compare them to our budget and to where we were last year. Everybody knows where they stand on there incentive program pay. I've gotten them all involved in the generation of income and probably have generated $2 to $3 million over the last two years. The last thing that we do every time is I pick one of the letters of the word and we talk about that word. And then during the month we reinforce it.

The Creative Solution

There were principles that I learned all through my many years of parochial school that I still carry with me and I plan to carry them with me. I believe that I have a high level of integrity and I'm an ethical person. I won't do something just to do it. I do things because [or only if] they're the right thing to do and that I have never succumbed to the pressure of having to meet a budget—and I don't ever intend to. I believe that I have my inner sanctum, which is that I want to be good to people and I believe that if you're good to people it comes back for you.

The Completion

I don't close the door here. The only thing we talk about that is, in my belief, confidential is an individual's performance—and that we close the doors for. Anything else the doors are open and everybody hears it. They are more likely to be threatened by something that they think is going on than if they see that the door is open all the time. Trust is a real big part of having people follow you where you want to take them. I mean I can develop the most brilliant vision that was ever developed but if my [people] don't trust me to take them where I say I'm going to, they're not going to follow me. They may pay me lip service but they're not going to implement the way they should.

Therefore, to truly empower teams for quality improvement, there must be a personal integrity and even a "systems integrity" in the way that we build and support Quantum Quality. Because integrity means "an alignment of what we think, say, and do," our actions and our organizational systems must be congruent with promoting and reinforcing what we believe and say about the importance of Quantum Quality .

This is the challenge posed in this book—and even more by Quantum Quality itself. As you take this journey toward Quantum Quality and seek to gain a creative edge for quality, remember two simple precepts:

Even the longest journey begins with a single step.

The process of getting there can be half the fun.

PART 2

The Mind-Set of Quantum Quality

4

Set Goals Beyond
Self-Interest

The humanistic aspect of our business is the product we offer—it helps customers monitor their blood glucose levels to maintain control and improve their quality of life. This is a motivating business. Service to our customer is paramount. Financial success is realized when customers receive proper attention.

—Emil Lojacono, vice president of quality assurance
and regulatory affairs, LifeScan, Inc., industry leader
in blood glucose monitoring devices for diabetics.

Mastering the Mind-Set

In the first stage of the Creative Journey (the Quantum Quality process), we establish the Challenge in two steps: (1) setting the purpose or goal and (2) describing the difficulty of accomplishing it. As shown in Figure 4.1, in this chapter, we'll address the QQ principle for step 1: Setting goals that are beyond our own self-interest.

What types of goals drive the growth and success of a company that is a consistent industry leader? The story of LifeScan, a Johnson & Johnson, exemplifies the dedication and commitment that is necessary for success. Emil Lojacono, vice president of quality, explains the foundation of LifeScan's business goals and objectives.

In 1981, LifeScan introduced a blood glucose meter (for diabetic patients) called GLUCOSCAN™. At this time, all meters were first-generation, which means that the product required a sequencing in steps for use: Wiping,

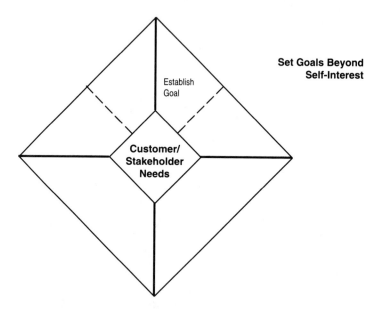

**4. THE
COMPLETION**

**1. THE
CHALLENGE**

Set Goals Beyond
Self-Interest

Establish
Goal

Customer/
Stakeholder
Needs

**3. THE
CREATIVE
SOLUTIONS**

**2. THE
FOCUS**

FIGURE 4.1.   The Creative Journey™

blotting, and timing. In 1987, LifeScan launched the one and only second generation product, ONE TOUCH® . This product simplified user procedures by eliminating wiping, blotting, and timing. After applying a drop of blood to the test strip, a blood glucose reading was available in just 45 seconds. In just months, the new ONE TOUCH® took the market by storm.

LifeScan's major competitors, who have been in the blood glucose monitoring industry longer than LifeScan, have just recently marketed a second generation product. LifeScan has offered this technology to its customers for more than five years.

In the spirit of continuous improvement, LifeScan launched the ONE TOUCHII® in February, 1991, following the original ONE TOUCH®. This more advanced product has features such as a nine-language LCD display indicating if the blood sample applied to the test strip is the proper amount and when the meter needs to be cleaned. These two functions assure accurate blood glucose readings.

The business of blood glucose monitoring is highly competitive. To Emil, at least three key factors are necessary for success in this business. The first factor is meter accuracy.

We sell accuracy to our customers. The ONE TOUCH® meter is the most accurate and reliable technology available today, and it has a very high level of customer acceptance. When I refer to our customers, I mean LifeScan's health care professionals, institutions, and the end-user diabetic patients. Today, LifeScan enjoys a 48 percent meter market share.

The second significant success factor is time-to-market.

LifeScan is a regulated company because we market a medical device that must comply with FDA submission requirements. Maintaining technological leadership is our key competitive advantage. LifeScan minimizes the time it takes to bring a product to market by utilizing fast cycle teams; adhering to the principles of pre-production quality assurance; and assuring timely and accurate submissions to the FDA.

The third and most crucial success factor is the one that Emil emphasizes the most—outstanding customer service.

We have a toll-free telephone number that is available to our customers 24 hours a day, seven days a week. Considering the health anomaly that our customers deal with, prompt service is critical. For example, if customers call and indicate a meter problem, we will replace the customer's meter within 24 hours. The returned meter will then be carefully inspected. LifeScan is a caring company whose focus is to meet our customers' needs "all the time."

There are many companies that aim for outstanding accuracy, timimg, and customer service. There are many companies that aim for product accuracy, reduced time-to-market and customer service. What does it take to have an entire organization align on this?

It takes dedication and commitment from top management. At LifeScan, caring makes the difference. We are a caring and sharing company, not just externally, but internally as well. People are working together in a participative environment that encourages individuality and respect. Top management demonstrates this philosophy to all areas of the company. We call it "walking the talk."

You become highly motivated when you know that your efforts will truly benefit the customer.

> *Our Quality Improvement Process (QIP) defines quality as "meeting customer requirements." During the first year of our QIP program, the person who logged in the greatest number of hours as a trainer was our company president. That's commitment!*

The principle of this chapter is a loaded one. Isn't the purpose of business to maximize what you earn—to focus on "What can I get?" rather than "What can I give?" Yet the shift from the former to the latter is one of the most fundamental keys to Quantum Quality and the full utilization of TQM tools.

There are five typical goals or "drivers" behind strategic initiatives for quality improvement: making money, beating competition, building one's organization/career, maximizing stockholder value, and meeting customer needs. Which is most fundamental to a business that wants to have sustainable advantage and market success? Does it make any real difference which one of these acts as the *primary* driving force?

I've asked these questions to a large number of executives, including Bill Lambert, who at the time was the senior manager of innovation resources at Proctor & Gamble Company.

> *Is our goal to increase profitability, or is increasing our profitability the outcome of reaching our goal of serving the consumer better than anyone else?" If our overarching purpose is to serve the consumer—to be the world's premier consumer products company in the areas in which we choose to compete—that will cause us to do very different things than if we focus just on beating the competition or focus just on achieving high levels of profitability.*
>
> *We certainly will invest more heavily up-front in understanding the consumer. We will certainly look at different relationships with our customers to streamline the flow of goods so that our consumers can get what they want, when they want it, and the way that they want it.*
>
> *Serving the customer is a win-win strategy. I believe it allows for other successful competitors to play the game. It doesn't say I have to beat them. Obviously if we serve the consumer better than anybody else, we will in fact, be number one. If we focus on cash-flow profitability and gauge our actions off of that end point solely, my guess is that we'll not wind up being number one or number two.*

Typically, we hear that making a profit, beating the competition, or giving shareholders a good return is the driver. Certainly, the corporate world is renowned for justifying decisions based on these criteria. Yet we're coming to understand that *only* the driver of *serving customers* can carry a business to sustainable, Deming-level or Baldrige-level quality and success over the long term.

In a workshop with a major computer hardware and software products company, I was working with the key managers and staff of their Northeast USA marketing organization. One team began working through the Creative Journey by writing a goal: "To maximize our revenues and profits." I asked them to consider an expanded version of that goal, based on "What are your goals in terms that would best serve and benefit your customers?" This led to a lot of head scratching, and then a lot of creativity. They ended up by describing the level of value and service they wished to provide their main customers, which would then lead to maximizing their revenues and profits.

This can be an empty exercise unless we recognize completely that in this and future ages, business success depends on defining our goals beyond our self-interest. Even in the case of this team, others in the organization said that this customer focus didn't really apply when the time was near for meeting their sales quotas. Instead of trying to develop solutions to customer problems, people were trying to convince customers that such-and-such a product was really what they needed.

Meeting customers needs—one of the four major dimensions of TQM, and potentially the most radical—is a key driver for business success. Other factors must be considered outcomes of that key strategic goal.

Yet Quantum Quality goes even beyond serving customers in two ways:

- QQ gets to the notion of customer *delight*.

- QQ goes beyond *customer* delight to consider serving all significant *stakeholders*.

As part of the mind-set of setting goals beyond self-interest, the key measure of "serving customers well" is no longer a matter of reducing customer complaints. Companies such as Proctor & Gamble and IBM are quickly discovering that there is a new hierarchy to service goals, which reverses the traditional order:

1. Actualizing personal potential (customer fulfilled)
2. Anticipating unstated wants (customer delighted)
3. Meeting known needs (customer satisfied)
4. Reducing complaints (customer not dissatisfied)

Most companies focus on the bottom two categories by reacting to changes after they happen. QQ companies are setting their sights on the top two in a creative, proactive way.

Customer delight is the key to Quantum Quality. It sees customers behave not in deficit terms ("Find a need and fill it") but in fulfillment terms ("Give them what will bring out their best"). For example, an advertisement for Eastman Kodak says, "Imagine the best day of your life. Now imagine living that way 365 days a year. That's how we define total quality at Kodak."

At LifeScan, Emil remarks:

We strive to "delight our customers." When you meet customer requirements, you are doing what is expected and anticipated. If you are delighting your customer, you are doing more than what is expected. Everyone at LifeScan, from the management board all the way into our organization, focuses on staying in touch with and delighting the customer.

We have a particular proactive philosophy that really delights the customer. Every month, each officer on the management board receives a list of customers to call and inquire about how they are doing. "Are they getting the service they need? Do they have any questions that we can answer further?" Our customers cannot imagine that someone at this level of management would take the time to make such a personal call, and the response is very positive. These calls exemplify doing whatever we can to literally meet the customers' requirements; and when you have an opportunity to exceed requirements, then you do it. This is how you really delight the customer.

Delight is a remarkable term to be emerging today, for it singles out a customer response—and an "emotive" one at that—as the measure of customer satisfaction. TQM has done a remarkable job of putting "customer" into our vocabulary, yet there is still more work needed to help people know how to focus their efforts toward delight and fulfillment.

And, delightfully, a focus on bringing out the best in a customer will also bring out the best in those who are providing the product or service! The vice president of design, worldwide, for Ford Motor Company, Jack Telnack, responded to this chapter's question about "primary driving force" by referring to the process of developing the extremely successful Taurus/Sable/Scorpio automobiles in the 1980s:

We had another edge to this process called BIC—Best in Class. We analyzed every part, every component of the car and compared each one with our competition and wanted to be better than our competition in every aspect of the car—I'm talking about switches, control knobs, steering wheels, seats . . . all the attention to detail, what we call "creature features" in the interior of the car. We wanted the customer to be surprised and delighted when they got in, so they had more than they expected when they originally purchased the car. I think this is what really clicked for us.

We are thus beginning to realize that what our companies do, sell, and throw away affects individuals as well as society as a whole. In the wake of our actions are waves of financial and social ramifications for the quality of life. When we make money the sole or primary goal rather than the *outcome* of providing high value for customers and other societal stakeholders, we often end up defeating the very success we strive for. Exploitation for profit creates a kind of "trade deficit" between energy and benefits.

Because business has historically operated in this financially focused way, people are now becoming very cynical, suspicious, and resistant to this "grab all you can" school of thought. As Emil Lojacono states,

The term "customer" has taken on a much broader meaning in today's business environment. In addition to our external and internal customers, we have an obligation to our other societal stakeholders. We must be aware of the impact that our business decisions make on our environment and be sensitive toward responsibilities to the communities in which we work and do business.

Customers and society's stakeholders are more sophisticated today. They demand more responsibility from business. And with Quantum Quality, we can go well beyond simply "putting up with" this state of affairs—we can applaud it! The new paradigm holds for us the prospect of feeling that we make a contribution, a difference, in the well-being of others. As product quality climbs and competitors find little margin for distinguishing themselves based on conformance to high standards, serving a customer well in his/her own eyes becomes the next creative edge.

Often we have work assignments that don't inspire us. We feel trapped into carrying out decisions we don't agree with. We feel no connection between what's important to us and what we do for a paycheck. We're caught adrift while, consciously or unconsciously, we wonder, "What's the purpose of my work, and how does it relate to my life? How do I make a real contribution here?"

Serving stakeholders doesn't have to be as heroic as saving lives. It's rather the intrinsic value we assign to a task, making a difference somehow, that gets us motivated, that gets us committed. This is the case whether it's filing reports, sweeping the floor at your place of worship, shelving books in a library, selling a candy bar to a customer, acting before the cameras, speaking to a convention, wiping the tear from a child's eye at a day care center, teaching algebra to school kids, driving a taxi, preparing a legal document, or what have you.

For Emil, this is a personal mind-set, not just "a nice thing to believe in."

When I interviewed with LifeScan, Jim Wilson, the president at that time (and currently president of Syntex), asked me, "What is more important, technical expertise or attitude?" My response was attitude *because attitude drives and motivates. Attitude toward business decisions and employees sets the atmosphere for an entire organization.*

I was really motivated when I worked for a division of Gillette that produced high volume hospital products such as transfusion devices and blood filters. It was a challengeing and a rewarding experience to make a product that helped people. I felt that if I did the best I possibly could, everything else would fall into place and that is exactly what happened.

I want to save money for my company and I feel a responsibility to do that, but in no way do I compromise what I deliver to my customer. Continuous improvement allows people to self-actualize; it is a feeling, a fulfillment.

Strengthening the System

One key to empowering quality teams in the Challenge stage is relating their goal(s) to the "big picture" of the organization as held by their sponsoring management. Another is to ensure there is sufficient delegation of responsibility and authority from those sponsors for the team to be able to take creative initiative.

To develop the culture for QQ, managers need to set up systematic ways in which these issues are consistently and frequently discussed, negotiated, and aligned. This will allow management to maintain linkage with the teams they empower, even if the teams are autonomous, self-managed, or cross-functional.

Therefore, *to set goals beyond self-interest*, sponsoring managers and team leaders need to dialogue and align themselves around two factors:

A. *Purpose/Vision*. This is the degree to which the team has goals that are important to them and that fit well with the sponsors' "big picture" strategy for the organization. When this is done well, the sponsors have built a consensus around a strategic vision; the team has a clear understanding of and belief in it and has developed a highly motivating project goal that is compatible with it.

B. *Roles/Authority.* This is the degree to which the team has the authority and leadership skills it needs to take initiative in achieving the goals. When this is done well, the team has sufficient authority for taking initiative, has strong "coaches" among its sponsors, has at least one person with strong skills for focusing and motivating the group, and has at least one person with strong skills for administration.

The key for both of these factors is beginning the empowerment process with people throughout the organization. Empowerment actually has three levels:

1. "Can do" attitude and skills
2. Sufficient authority to take initiative in handling creative challenges
3. Alignment with people and systems in the organization

No one can empower us at the first level; we are responsible for our attitude and skill development. At the second level it takes a courageous, "can do" person to want the authority, and a courageous manager to be willing to empower people, to let go of control. Ed McCracken, CEO of Silicon Graphics, comments:

> *I split Silicon Valley into companies where management's primary job is to say "yes" and companies where the primary job seems to be to say "no." It's amazing how most of the old line companies now have management set up to say, "No, you can't do that for these reasons." I think it is really important for management to be able to say "Yes, we can do that and I'll help you." That's what management is all about.*
>
> *We have such bright, good people in our company. In most cases, I act as a cheerleader or a coach—then I get out of the way. It takes much more balance to manage this way than it takes to make the right decision. A lot of CEOs actually believe that they make all the decisions in the company.*
>
> *You are, in some greater sense, responsible for everything, but believing that you are in control of what goes on in a company of 3,400 people with thousands of customers is silly. You aren't. You can nudge people here and there and you can capture the energy around you and imbed it in your products and programs, but that's about it.*

As sponsors and teams align on these two issues, they will foster a culture in which they collaborate well to identify mutually reinforcing goals. Strategic visioning, guided visualizations, and stakeholder-focused MBO are some of the tools that can help institutionalize this aspect of a positive sponsor-team relationship.

Practicing the Paradigm

Learning

As mentioned in the Introduction, Quantum Quality revolves around many "living questions"—for which there will be only "answers for now" as conditions change. The key question that organizes the dimension of *learning* in the Challenge stage is "What's inspiring?"

TQM already focuses on learning what's important to accomplish for a customer. There's also the issue of learning what's important for stakeholders: employees, managers, society, the environment, and so on.

In order to effectively ask, answer, and re-ask that question from many perspectives, we need to learn to inquire and to listen well. Patricia Moore, former manager of consulting services at Hewlett-Packard, takes a skillful approach to learning what will make a difference:

> A good leader isn't necessarily the one who originates the idea of purpose or direction or vision. They're often the ones who listen so well they're able to capture the threads that come from their constituents, their customers, etc., and they're able to recognize it. "What is it our customers want from us? What is their definition of value? How are they trying to serve their customers?" All of that is service.

Eventually, we must take this question, "What's inspiring?" and learn how to

(A) develop commitment to a compelling purpose and vision
(B) use an effective range of leadership roles and initiative

To ingrain these questions into the fabric of a truly innovative learning organization, we must inventively communicate our notions of the most meaningful, motivating goals and identify the people who most naturally want to take the leadership initiative to actualize the goals, whatever his or her job position might be.

In addition, there is a level of personal inquiry that can help us learn more about ourselves and enable us to discover how quality improvement can be an intrinsically satisfying way of working and living. For example, we can ask ourselves, "What are the most inspiring work challenges I've ever handled; what do they have in common that I'd like to build into any work challenge I face?" Or even, "What is my sense of purpose in life and how can I express that through my work?"

The answers to these questions invariably lead us to higher levels of motivation, meaning, risk taking, and initiative. This level of commitment is part and parcel to the new paradigm of and mind-set of Quantum Quality. Then we can feel and say to ourselves, "We *do* make a difference!"

Values

Why would anyone give the best possible service if no one is watching—if no one reinforced the behavior with a bonus, a promotion, or even a pat on the back? What, in these cases, would make service something that is intrinsically motivating?

By asking such questions, we can drive our insights deeper toward the level of basic human nature. We can discover some very fundamental human values that are intrinsically motivating because they tap into the connectedness and community that is natural to the human condition. We are all part of a larger whole—we are born that way, we'll die that way, and we can best live in recognition of that fact.

One answer to the question is that a person would give service even if no one were looking out of a sincere concern for others' well being. When we tap into our concern for our own, personal well being, we may naturally choose to serve others without experiencing a sense of self-sacrifice. It can even be a great pleasure.

This is quite easy to see in the story of the HP assembly person who found a resonance between the purpose of her work and her deepest personal values. Those personal values are the key to cultivating that mutual commitment. When we can make a link between our personal values, our job assignments, and the spirit with which we do our job, all sorts of miracles can happen.

Beyond self-interest means doing what has heart and meaning. Heartfelt, meaningful action comes in when we reach beyond ourselves to our sense of natural connection with others, to make a contribution. With values such as service and well-being, we can develop a selfless caring that diminishes our egos, expands our deeper self, and leads us to the true driver of sustainable business success. We can find greater meaning and motivation in the challenges we choose, for the victories we strive for will be as much inner challenges as outer ones.

Creativity

Even though innovation may seem to occur by happenstance, it more than ever needs to be targeted and directed. In pharmaceuticals, for example, R&D no longer looks just to discovering the behavior of certain compounds and turning them into drugs; companies are inventing molecules and designing them to behave in prescribed ways.

Without a clear sense of a target, the passionate pursuit of quality improvement can be scattered—efficient at the individual or team level, yet wasteful and disorganized at the company level.

Innovation requires more than just creative ideas; successful implementation of the best ideas is just as important. A team has to creatively synthesize those ideas and craft a goal statement to make sure that each party could agree, "Yes, that's a compelling goal from my point of view."

Sustainability

A key factor for the sustainable growth of a company, a country, and the global market is *taking responsibility for the whole.* Taguchi defines quality in terms of the contribution we make to society, not just in terms of the benefit to the company or its customers. The earth's environment is an important stakeholder that is part of this whole.

When Deming and Juran first started preaching the quality gospel, the conventional wisdom said that high quality costs money. When they showed that high quality actually saved money, people woke up. The same issue is at stake with making wise ecological decisions: They don't have to cost money—they can save it.

To effectively implement this first QQ principle (set goals beyond self-interest), a team must demand from each member that he/she honestly identify and tap into the reservoir of well-being we can all feel when we expand beyond our own personal concerns.

Emil Lojacono concludes,

> *The other factor that impacts everything we do is LifeScan's global perspective. Within our company, we have cultures representing almost every part of the world. We strive to learn not only about each other, but also about how to manage cultural/global diversity while growing at such a phenomenal rate.*

Based on the well-known slogan, "Think globally, act locally," the demand at this first step in the Quantum Quality process is to think globally.

5

Manage Uncertainty Rather than Minimize Risk

In the 1970s, companies like ours required 10 years to make a tenfold increase in the performance of a computer system. In the 1980s, the tenfold increase became possible in 7 years. Now it's 3.5 years.

Every time computer performance changes by 100 times, a fundamental usage paradigm shift occurs. Computers become obsolete because the way systems are designed and used changes radically. This means absolute chaos in our industry. But it also means that there is tremendous opportunity to be at the leading edge of new markets.

We try to learn about the new paradigms first. We try to integrate these new ideas into our new computer systems and into the way we do business.

—Ed McCracken, CEO of Silicon Graphics (industry leader in computer workstations)

Mastering the Mind-Set

In the first stage of Quantum Quality's Creative Journey, in addition to establishing the goal or vision, we must deal with the difficulty of accomplishing it. As shown in Figure 5.1, in this chapter we'll address the principle for tackling this difficulty in a Quantum Quality way: Managing uncertainty rather than minimize risk.

At first, the ideal of minimizing risk may seem to be the most natural, advisable, rational way to deal with the vast uncertainty and change we face daily. The paradox is that the very attempt to minimize risk can and does lead to strategies and behaviors that actually *increase* the level of risk in which we place ourselves. Thus, the term "managing uncertainty" is offered here as an alternative, to be explored as a QQ principle in two ways:

- Managing uncertainty in strategic business planning
- Managing uncertainty at the personal level

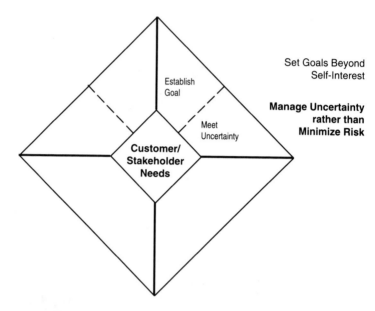

4. THE
COMPLETION

1. THE
CHALLENGE

3. THE
CREATIVE
SOLUTIONS

2. THE
FOCUS

FIGURE 5.1.   The Creative Journey™

Strategic Planning and Action

It's no wonder that people feel that "business is warfare." Not only is it the model many of us grew up with—even in terms of organizational structure and management—but also we're currently experiencing a state of affairs comparable to a state of war: rapid change, vast uncertainty, and lack of control of events. Surveys of CEOs conducted over the past decade have consistently revealed concerns about:

- Fierce competition—domestic, international, and cross-industry
- Deregulation of industries—competition, changing markets, and industry restructuring
- Changing markets—market segmentation, consumer values, and offshore markets

- Economic/financial uncertainty—growth/stability, inflation/interest rates, capital availability, and the international monetary system
- Government policies/uncertainty—taxation, trade, regulation, and political risk
- Technological impacts on business—tracking and timing of investments
- Changing workforce—productivity, education/training, and succession planning

How does a company turn this turbulence into an advantage, even in an industry best known for its severe competitiveness and rapid product turnover? Ed McCracken, CEO of Silicon Graphics, gives us some clues.

> *We probably have the least organized quality improvement program of any of the computer workstation manufacturers; yet, we came out number one in customer satisfaction every quarter last year (according to Dataquest surveys). Why is that? By adapting best to the way the world is changing. So many of the quality programs are about making minor improvements to old paradigms.*
>
> *We value our best and brightest customers—LucasFilm developing new movies, NASA designing new types of aircraft. Our brightest designers work with our most advanced customers to determine what the market will want 18 months into the future. By delivering quickly with short cycle-time engineering, we create tremendous levels of customer satisfaction.*
>
> *For example, three years ago, I was in Japan visiting the head of computer engineering for one of the automotive companies. I asked, "What can we do to better serve your needs?" He sat on the edge of his chair and said, "We need your computer to be ten times more powerful in both computing and graphics." Then he went on to describe how they would change their entire engineering process if their workstations were faster.*
>
> *Since that time, we have delivered systems that are ten times more powerful and they are in the process of doing their designs in different, more team-oriented ways. Those customers who help us to define a new paradigm are very valuable.*

We're being called upon to deal with such situations in a mobilized and holistic frame of mind, to synthesize and find unity in diversity, rather than to attack and destroy. For example, the 1980s and 1990s have introduced the era of strategic alliances—IBM with Apple Computer and GM with Toyota—as evidence of the practical nature of forming cooperative ventures with competitors. Even the TQM emphasis on customer–supplier–company relationships is evolving: It's not a matter of balancing competing interests, but of growing a mutual-interest community!

To define a strategic vision relevant in today's world, we must address four major questions: "What do we want to be?" "What does the world want us to be?" "What are we capable of being?" "What are we called to be?" If any of these questions is not seriously addressed, an organization can seriously lose its balance:

- To ask only, "What do we want to be?" often results in a cocoon of product development typical of the technology-driven firm that develops something in R&D and then asks marketing to find a customer.

- To ask only, "What does the world want us to be?" often results in a scatterbrained reactivity to market trends.

- To ask only, "What are we capable of being?" can limit our dreams to our *current* strengths and weaknesses.

- To ask only, "What are we called to be?" can burn out staff who overinvest their enthusiasm in unachievable goals.

Given the rapid pace of change in the planning horizon, there are two approaches for using these questions to develop strategic plans and to introduce "on-time" new products, services, and work methods. One is to be very good at short-term horizons and quick-to-market solutions. The other is to abandon forecasts and use environmental scenarios for long-term planning.

Ed McCracken follows the first approach.

We don't believe in long-term planning. We believe in creating options for the future and working with customers to implement what we can see in front of our nose over the next 18 months, do that very quickly, and then get on to the next thing. So we try not to get wedded to technologies or even a way that customers use things.

Ed directs the risks the company will take by creating "solution spaces" within which individuals and teams can take initiative in finding new paradigm solutions in rapid time.

If somebody proposes something for the banking industry, I'm not going to be very excited about it because we're not in the banking industry. Our solution space requires innovation, so if someone proposes a new program or product that doesn't have much innovation in it, then it is outside the solution space. So that's a problem. I communicate our solution space to our team at program reviews by talking to people in the halls, at all Hands Meetings, or at communication sessions with employees. As long as projects are within that large solution space, I'm happy, and I don't need to micromanage.

The other approach to staying on top of rapid change is to alter the long-term planning mode. Carlene Ellis, a corporate vice president and officer for Intel Corporation, has altered the way Intel conducts its strategic planning.

Planning has become our technique for just-in-time business, but it doesn't come from just doing strategic planning as an event, which hi-tech firms are famous for. Putting together a two-hour presentation is clearly not a long-range plan. I asked the executives, "Do you want a long range vision that people can get . . . or do you want presentations? Let's decide what we want."

We could event-drive a plan and then all of a sudden Andy Grove (CEO) would ask, "Why aren't we doing what we said we were going to do?" The Baldrige judges said in their report, you appear to be very tuned in to the need for a vision, you clearly were rigorous on the detail, but you're disconnected.

We came up with something we call Management by Planning, which we implemented in '89, '90, very painfully. And, it's an integrated whole that runs year round. In January, we take an external view of the world. In March we look at an environmental scan of Intel and ask, "What's changed?" Then, about May, June, we do the updating of the long-range plan. About July, August, we update the product-line business plan, which is merged into the long-range plan. By December, we're starting all over.

If a lightning bolt came out of the sky in June, called competitors, right then we'd pretend it's January; the environmental stand has changed. It allows for huddling. It's kind of fun seeing that change at Intel through the years. The out-of-the-box mentality and the sharing of this vision, where everyone's heart light comes on, is what it's all about.

Risk taking is not a goal in itself; it's something usually needed to achieve the goal. As mentioned at the outset of this chapter, techniques for risk management and budget planning are often aimed to minimize risk; yet in times of high uncertainty, they inadvertently promote high-risk decision making because they inhibit creative, proactive changes in strategy and operations that are needed to keep up with the changing environment.

To *manage uncertainty*, there are many tools for assessing risk and strategizing how to prepare for risk. Companies such as Royal Dutch Shell have practiced specific skills and techniques, such as scenarios-based planning, for developing creative midcourse corrections and making the right decisions to be *positioned* to excel even in uncertain times.[1]

Ironically, forecast-based planning is the more traditional yet more risky approach; because it "bets the company's future" on a single view of what the future industry environment will be. Scenario-based planning is more nontraditional yet more conservative, in that it provides a safer basis for developing strategy(ies) that will provide growth no matter which alternative future emerges.

This juxtaposition of traditional-and-risky versus nontraditional-and-conservative is the paradox that people face everywhere in staying with the older paradigms of management versus moving into innovative, new modes of management that are more fitting to the 1990s! The call to "manage uncertainty" is not a call for taking more risks or bigger risks or less-prudent risks. Just the opposite, it's a call to wake up to when traditional forms of minimizing risk have the consequences of taking unnecessary risks.

Personal Initiative and Risk

As important as these planning tools are, just as important are personal insights into (1) our comfort levels with risk and (2) what leads us to take initiative. Risk taking is something that is first encountered in the Challenge stage of the Creative Journey, yet risks occur *throughout* the Journey.

According to Dave Ehlen, CEO of Wilson Learning Corporation, one of the largest providers of corporate training materials in the world, the big issue is, "What gives a person or team the courage and skills to stand up and make a difference? What provides the boost and the competence for taking the right risks?" He goes on to say, "Even the best efforts of an extraordinary innovative team can be undermined without the buy-in of senior management, systems that support the initiative, and a good fit with the existing corporate culture."[2]

---

[1] Tools such as scenario planning and vulnerability analysis, as well as scanning and monitoring systems, are described in William C. Miller, *The Creative Edge* (Boston: Addison-Wesley, 1987).

[2]*Telemarketing*, Oct. 1992, pages 59–62, Norwalk, CT.

Our willingness to take initiative is influenced by having (or creating) meaningful challenges, high self-esteem, confidence in our innovativeness, and a willingness to measure success by *learning* as well as achievement. On this last point, if there is high-quality decision making with all available information, then the possibility of not achieving a goal—having what Frank Carrubba of HP Labs called "intelligent failure"—must be acceptable. The myth of "perfect competency" must be punctured to allow people to say "I don't know" when assessing the risks associated with a quality challenge. Measurement and rewards systems for individuals and teams have a great deal to do with whether someone makes decisions by hiding behind "what the numbers say" or if they take responsibility for their comfort level with risk and ambiguity. Those systems will be specifically addressed in Chapter Eleven.

The ever-so-common personal fear of failure, or even fear of success,[3] is a key variable in whether we always strive to minimize risk, to hold on to predictability, rather than position ourselves across the domains of uncertainty.

Silicon Graphics was founded to build systems around custom silicon chips that contained our own unique graphics algorithms. About six years ago, one of our best young designers, Kurt Akeley, devised a new way of doing graphics using a much simpler approach with parts you could buy off-the-shelf from other companies. You can imagine how our engineering leaders reacted because it violated the principles upon which the company was founded.

We had a one-week argument. The people involved met every day in a conference room. Each day they would present technical arguments to each other. At the end of the week, the young engineer won, and we did it his way. He was tremendously successful. Kurt is now one of the vice presidents of Silicon Graphics.

This is one of the culture-defining stories in our company. Kurt was willing to take the risk. He was willing to fight for an entirely different way of doing things. He won for technical, pragmatic reasons. The person who won had the best ideas, not the organizational power.

---

[3] See Chapter Twelve for an example of "too much success" almost causing business failure.

Kurt took a risk, to be sure. As Ed McCracken says:

> *The greatest fear is not financial loss, but embarrassment in front of our peers, competitors, subordinates, or management.*

A company might get hurt one year, but year in and year out, whether a manager makes or loses money, doesn't inhibit risk taking as much as the fear of being embarrassed. We all may have grown up with some degree of what I call a "prove it" pattern. There is little satisfaction, as if we are continually driven to be more, do more, get more. This is often accompanied by the (childhood?) message, "You're not worth anything until you prove yourself!"

Trying to avoid embarrassment, to win others' approval, to fill this emptiness inside leads to performance anxiety and attempts to dominate. All the inherently "conditional" forms of getting approval (from ourselves as well as from others) are bound to fail, because *no* work can provide the sense of unconditional worth we're all looking for in the first place. And when it does fail, feelings of betrayal often arise (in reality, betrayal by one's own belief system of low self-esteem) . . . sometimes leading to expressions of depressed resignation or angry dominance.

We all face dark times during our careers, such as job layoffs, reorganizations, racism and sexism in job promotions, and new job requirements based on new economic conditions. We all face the demon in another way, in the temptations to benefit from injustices: grabbing the perks for privileged employee groups, accepting a promotion that was based unfairly on sex or race discrimination, exploiting consumers for another dollar.

Both types of challenges require us to tap into our character—our deepest sense of the best human values, such as honesty and dignity, caring and compassion, wholeness and integrity. From these we begin to gain the confidence that we can rise to the challenge, whatever it is, and find success.

By this type of process (which is dealt with in more detail in the next chapter), we not only become more victorious, we grow into greater spiritual maturity. There truly is a basis for saying that each situation is presented to us for our progressing toward greater experience, power, love, and wisdom as we live and work.

From a sense of wholeness, we can embrace the challenges we face, rather than sinking back into the past from a fear of risk. This doesn't imply foolish decisions. In fact, with wholeness, we are closer to our inherent wisdom, so we make even wiser choices about which risks are worthy and which aren't. A climate of fear leads to compliance, whereas a climate of confidence leads to commitment.

Strengthening the System

In addition to the factors outlined in the previous chapter—Purpose/ Vision and Roles/Authority—two more factors for empowering quality teams in the challenge stage are: understanding the variables and unknowns in the business environment; and clarifying the key success factors for operating in that environment.

That is, *to manage uncertainty rather than minimize risk,* sponsoring managers and team leaders can set up systematic ways in which the following factors are also frequently discussed, negotiated, and aligned, to strengthen the linkage between them:

C. *Business/Technology Environment.* This is the degree to which the team and the sponsors understand the business and technology issues in the same way. When this is done well, the team understands the sponsors' view of the current business/technology environment (using vulnerability analysis, customer needs assessments, and other tools), has ways to assess the uncertainty of any forecast, has strong contacts with its customers, and is active in gathering information on its areas of expertise.

D. *Key Success Factors.* This is the degree to which the team and the sponsors have the same understanding of the critical business factors for serving the customers and the organization. When this is done well, the team understands its sponsor's definitions of business success for the organization as a whole, has defined the success factors for their project, has assessed the risks for the organization and for each person in the group.

As sponsors and teams align on these two issues, they will foster a culture in which they continually understand the same context and importance for achieving their goals. Multiple scenarios, vulnerability analysis, and customer-needs analysis are some of the tools that can help institutionalize this aspect of a positive sponsor-team relationship.

Practicing the Paradigm

Learning

As we've seen, the key question that stimulates and organizes learning in the Challenge stage is "What's inspiring?" That includes not only "What goal are we striving for?" but also "What is the *context* that gives importance to this goal?"

Chapter Four stated that in learning about "What goal are we striving for?" we must develop our skills in

(A) developing commitment to a compelling purpose and vision
(B) using an effective range of leadership roles and styles

To learn about the context for that goal, we must learn how to

(C) stay up to date on what's going on outside the organization (customers, technology, etc.)
(D) understand the keys to the organization's success

To set appropriate strategic direction, we all need to combine purpose and vision with understanding the external environment; the gusts and waves of changing social, economic, competitor, technological, environmental, political, and human conditions.

There are two approaches to gathering information about the external environment: scanning and monitoring. Scanning is an early warning system used to detect signals of new trends of potential importance to the organization. Monitoring is the detailed tracking of events and trends of known importance to the organization. A system for scanning and monitoring not only ensures that an organization has up-to-date information about trends of known importance, but also keeps it from being surprised by new trends.

To institutionalize this and foster the learning organization, we can work with different tools for scanning, monitoring, and analyzing customer needs, economic trends, vulnerability analysis, and such. In addition, we can develop ways to communicate the key trends and keys to success in this fast-changing world to everyone in the organization. This demands an level of openness about the information that is gathered, but without this openness, there will be no true learning by those who must directly respond to quality/customer/stakeholder concerns. This is a key to turning a collection of individuals who learn into a learning organization.

For example, Toshiba has a staff of full-time junior managers to monitor its business environment worldwide, analyze and condense the information, and distribute it throughout the organization. Even supervisors and professional staff have direct access to this information. They are stimulated by it to think of new, innovative ways of doing business. At a minimum, they understand more fully the context behind many executive decisions that might otherwise appear arbitrary, such as the introduction of cost-cutting measures or the funding of one project but not another. In fast-moving markets, this broad participation in innovation can be the primary competitive advantage of your organization.

In addition, there's further personal inquiry that will help us learn about ourselves—and to discover in that learning how quality can be an intrinsically satisfying way of work and life. For example, we can ask ourselves, "How comfortable am I when I face a great deal of ambiguity— when do I feel anxious and rush into action, and when do I work more deliberately, with confidence?" Or we can ask, "How curious and willing am I to find out about the world outside of my immediate concerns—will I allow that extra complexity into my work?" The answers to these questions invariably lead us to higher levels of tolerance in the face of challenges that can induce high levels of anxiety. Then we can feel, "We're stimulated by uncertainty and challenge."

Values

In Chapter Four, we saw that one answer to the question "Why would a person give great service when no one is looking?" is: *out of a sincere caring for others' well-being.* When we tap into our own level of concern for well-being, we naturally choose to serve others.

The same answer comes up when we ask, "Why would a person take a risk?" (given some degree of uncertainty of accomplishing a goal). Risk is felt in direct relationship to a concern for well-being. It's our definition of what well-being means that determines our risk-aversive or risk-taking tendencies. Both can stem from caring for the well-being of ourselves and others ("beyond self-interest").

Even the fear of taking risks is based on a concern for our well-being and wholeness. At issue is whether we have superficially defined our well-being as "lack of embarrassment" or "avoiding looking foolish." Or, in other words, if we have defined well-being purely in terms of self-interest rather than a more open caring for other's interests (and well-being) as well as (or instead of) our own.

Applying the deep human value of well-being to discussions of risk and uncertainty can bring a deep sense of "heartful" meaning and value to the dialogue, for from the core of our heart (*cœur*) will come the *cour*age we need in this era of rapid change.

Creativity

Benchmarking does more than just calibrate how well others (competitors) have done with a certain technology, process, or what have you—demonstrating how urgent is the need for leaping ahead rather than falling (further) behind. Perhaps it's primary purpose is to stimulate people to reach *beyond* what they have done, to know that they can apply their creativity to do things better or differently.

And as Greg Watson, vice president of quality at Xerox reminds us:

The concept of benchmarking in quality changes the business paradigm from one of competition to one of increased cooperation. Years ago Macy's and Gimbel's were the two major department stores in New York. Macy's would do whatever they had to gain competitive advantage over Gimbel's. That two-store competition epitomizes the old business theory—competitors don't cooperate. Yet, assessing their results today, Gimbel's went bankrupt about ten years ago and Macy's is fighting to maintain their margins. Perhaps there were areas where cooperation would have ended up in the best interest of both organizations and society at large. Of course, we will have to adjust our nation's industrial policy and antitrust laws to gain an environment of increased cooperation among competitors—it is easier to build a business relationship with a Japanese competitor than an American competitor because business relationships are not uniformly legislated worldwide. Talk about an additional cost to society caused by a restriction upon the innovative process imposed by our government!

However, if improperly implemented, benchmarking can have a down side: limiting people's thinking, to reach only for being the "best benchmark" rather than aiming even beyond those limits to "the best we can be." Properly applied benchmarking would project performance to a future point in time and use a challenge goal to drive performance to the new benchmark.

Sustainability

Another aspect of sustainability is focusing on *fulfilling purpose and potential* rather than meeting deficit needs. Professor S. K. Chakraborty of the Indian Institute of Management in Calcutta has provided insights into the western assumptions about motivation.

> *No matter what innovative labels are attached to the various propellants of human activity, all these authors (Maslow, McGregor, Herzberg, Likert, Hersey, Blanchard) seem to conceive of man as a package of wants—the needs of organizational members.*[4]

For Dr. Chakraborty, the "giving" model of man, to the contrary, emphasizes the discipline and spirituality of serving others, beyond one's self interest, and thereby fostering sustained economic affluence.

> *Between "true" self interest and social interest, no intrinsic conflict is visualized in Indian thought. Hence, the giving model really does not imply that the individual is a mere sacrificial goat on the altar of society. Even if there is an apparent loss to an individual by willingly giving or sacrificing for others, there is bound to be real gain to him—both psychologically (which includes the spiritual aspect) and materially (ibid).*

Fear is based on projections of "failure to meet one's needs" and being attached to attaining one's desires. Fear poses a deficit-driven understanding of motivation: we are moved to fill up what we lack, and to avoid creating a lack. Even the business maxim "Find a need and fill it" is based on a deficit model of motivation. Managers that motivate by fear believe that productivity happens when people want to avoid a lack (of jobs, etc.) or fill up a hole in their lives (with money, etc.).

Fear-based decisions will focus on how to cut up the "limited pie" of economic benefits, rather than on how to create a newer or bigger pie to share. Deficit thinking puts us into a "dog-eat-dog" frame of mind that minimizes the potential advantages from any quality program, especially QQ. Fear leads to short-term horizons for defining situations as problems, a working to solve problems and meet needs.

---

[4] S. K. Chakraborty, *Managerial Effectiveness and Quality of Worklife* (New Delhi: Tata McGraw-Hill, 1987).

There is an alternative. Motivation can be seen as the fulfillment of one's sense of purpose and potential. Rather than a lack of something, we are fulfilled and complete and whole as we already are, and will continue to grow into what we can next become. [5]

Fulfillment-driven psychology, rather than the needs-driven psychology, leads to *long-term sustainability* horizons for recognizing opportunities and potential, and bringing the best solutions forward.

Ed McCracken sums up how to incorporate the mind-set of managing uncertainty:

> *It's pretty obvious that in many cases the riskiest thing you can do is to do nothing. The most powerful thing anyone can do to improve performance for a business is to build trust. Increased trust in an organization will result in improved performance. With trust comes a feeling of personal safety. And with safety, people are willing to take a risk.*
>
> *I have the old quote on my workstation: "All independent thought, new ideas or endeavors beyond the common measure are greeted with disapproval, ranging from skepticism and ridicule to violent outrage."[6] You have to overcome this. If people take risk, there turns out to be not very much risk at all, and that's when you start to get the major shifts.*

---

[5] The analogy of a rose bush comes to mind: A young rose bush, standing 2 feet tall with a dozen flowers, is still 100 percent a rose bush; it is not incomplete! Yet is can still grow into a 4-foot-tall bush with two dozen flowers, growing according to its purpose and potential.

[6] See also the discussion of Silicon Graphics in Richard A. Shaffer, "Scientific Computing," *Forbes*, Sept. 28, 1992, p. 142.

6

Make Staff Development a Two-Way Street

We needed to take it another step, rather than just making another process or work-flow change. Personally, I needed the workplace to be different for me—one I looked forward to being involved with—and I felt that I couldn't be the only person who felt this way. So that's what we've done.

—Suzanne Mamet, second vice president, Travelers Insurance Corporation, Information Systems Department

- *It's management. I know them so much better and trust them. This helps me greatly. I know they'd back me up. I know what risks are acceptable, and I feel confident taking them.*
- *Whoa! There's an epidemic of sanity starting to stir.*

—Data Administration Staff members

Mastering the Mind-Set

In the second stage of the QQ proccess, the Focus Stage, we begin working on the Challenge in two steps: tapping into our character (to gain confidence in meeting the challenge) and analyzing the key issues and priorities for improvement. As shown in Figure 6.1, in this chapter we'll address the principle for tapping into character in a Quantum Quality way: Making staff development a two-way street.

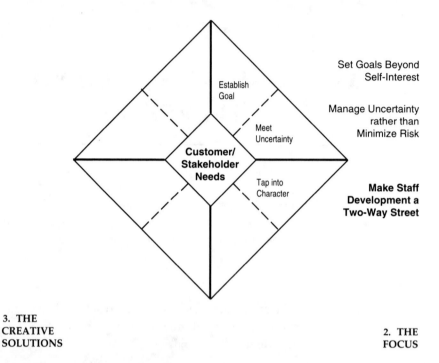

**4. THE
COMPLETION**

**1. THE
CHALLENGE**

Establish
Goal

Set Goals Beyond
Self-Interest

Meet
Uncertainty

Manage Uncertainty
rather than
Minimize Risk

**Customer/
Stakeholder
Needs**

Tap into
Character

**Make Staff
Development a
Two-Way Street**

**3. THE
CREATIVE
SOLUTIONS**

**2. THE
FOCUS**

FIGURE 6.1.   The Creative Journey™

Suzanne's department serves The Traveler's centralized data-process-ing group. They were part of a team that completed a very difficult, expensive, and complex initiative to support the development of applica-tions that were really pushing the boundaries of technology.

The key technical challenge was dealing with enormous-size relational data bases in the medical claims area. We had two projects like that with the same manager from our organization involved. And we were very successful in one and struggled in the other.

The key to the one team's success was that, from the beginning, it was more open to working in a different way, functioning as one team with the customer, and not as a separate support organization with synthetic barriers about who does what. The data administration staff of 100 tech-nical professionals originally had the opportunity to go through a special training program[1] where people learned about themselves, how to take care of one another as a team, and how to focus on their customers.

Everyone in the data administration group bought into a common purpose and was willing to let everyone play the role they could best play without creating artificial boundaries.

People developed a sense of trust with each other so that they were able to reveal more of who they really were. We've created a spirit of an organization of people who help each other, an organization with a great deal of flexibility to manage "impermanent change." We've got a group that's much more comfortable in saying, "Let's see how we should be organized and who we should be" rather than "Who's going to be in charge and who reports to whom. . . ." It's more open, it's more sharing, and it helps respond to the business needs where we need to try things.

In any team there are always issues that come up, at times people emotionally taking advantage of other team members. Instead of people just being resentful and creating isolation on the team, we've been able to sit down and address those things. We opened up a lot and really established the climate where we can deal with tough issues and resolve them easily as a team, where everyone comes out feeling good.

Given this strength of character of the data administration organization, they were able to reach out to their customer base and find new ways of working together.

We held about ten or eleven customer-focus sessions to give them a chance to tell us what they needed from us, how they needed to work, how they wanted to work with us, and how they could tell us when we successfully met their expectations. Even in the sessions that started out as a customer attack, when they saw the spirit in which it was being done, and we really wanted to listen without defending ourselves, every session came out in a very constructive way.

To do that, there had to be a greater sense of internal confidence in being able to be open to hearing messages that were suggestive of improvement—to shift from a defensive position to one where we said our job basically is to support our customers in the way they like best—to be open enough to be able to say, "Tell us how you want to work with us." And we evolved.

We collected thirty items, and now we are developing action plans on how to address each of those. One key thing we changed was asking our customers

---

[1] Conducted by InnerWork Technologies, Inc., of Seattle and Philadelphia.

up front before they call us, to please get us involved early in efforts so we can point out things that help us be more prepared—a totally different style.

Also, when we do something for our customers, we call them and let them know that we've done it and ask them to check it out, and we ask them, "Was this handled in a way that worked well for you? Can you suggest any changes?" And that is an enormous shift in how we were working.

The results of this staff development have been demonstrated in many ways. Dr. Richard Wagner of the University of Wisconsin (Whitewater) Graduate School of Business is a nationally known expert in independently measuring corporate change efforts. He headed up research on the changes in the productivity and effectiveness of the team. Both the range and the degree of shifts on fifteen indicators show that something profound has occurred.

I've rarely seen a project seek to make such fundamental improvements in both people and the work environment. The post-test measurements are outstanding and we've looked at over 20,000 change program participants. Nearly every measure went up in statistically significant ways.

For instance, two behavioral indicators—"risk taking" and "locus of control" ("I control my own success at work")—which rarely showed any post-test changes in previous UW studies, had significantly changed. So did measures on the deeper levels of trust, stress mastery, mental fitness, group bonding, honesty, management support, fun, commitment, problem solving, empowerment, feedback, and vision. Also, post-tests that were conducted over a six-month time-span showed these statistically significant results being maintained, or even increasing in some cases.

The reason is that there is a sense of values, of making commitments to each other, and of building trust. The employment contract that they were looking for was, "How can I develop more of who I am, more of my being, and help others develop as well?" Now there is a partnership among these people because they are speaking to their deepest values and what they reallly want out of life and out of work.

Bill Carroll, a member of the team, explains this level of team spirit.

The principles we're applying give us a picture of a new way we can live and work. It's an inside-out approach to change. If managers ask, "How do you get work done more efficiently with a better end-product?" I tell them, "Along with improving the work process, build trust, communicate honestly, support each team member, and find ways to drive out fear. Relearn the idea that it's important for everyone to seek balance and wholeness in and through work. When this catches fire, an epidemic of sanity—even love—can spread.

As Suzanne Mamet summarizes, the benefits flow to everyone.

Customers are really going out of their way more than ever before to send me messages about people in my organization—about their attitude, about their helpfulness.

We're also giving awards to our customers for being good customers, which has been remarkable, too. They're rather shocked. It's just something that nobody ever did.

The old work ethic—"Work hard, do what you're told, work here for the rest of your life, be loyal . . . and we'll take care of you"—has been disappearing. Just look at the levels of job switching and at the levels of "betrayed" workers when plants close to get a few signs of the times.

A new work ethic has grown up to replace it. The movement toward more employee participation and involvement reflects a trend of giving and taking more personal responsibility for decisions.

This sense of responsibility is aligned with the U.S.'s history of entrepreneurial spirit, though not with bureaucratic management. It values deep personal expression, including our deepest, most motivating values as well as our talents. To tap into this spirit, to truly gain a sense of personal success, we must bring these values to the fore.

In this arena, there are two issues we all face: "How do we get the best from ourselves and those we work with?" and "How do we maintain commitment and loyalty at a time when it feels like everyone is exploiting everyone else?"

When recruiting new staff, the days are gone when an executive might hire people in their 20s and expect them to stay with the company unitl retirement. One can then say, "If you come to work for us, I'll expect that some day, you won't be working for me or even the company anymore. Anticipating that, my commitment to you is that when you leave, I will have done my best to see that you've grown professionally and, I hope, personally."

That's what I've begun to call "the two-way street" at work. We develop ourselves to make a stronger contribution in our work. And we use our work as a vehicle to develop ourselves. Then and only then do we get committed to our work. Ideally, there's a two-way contract for staff development: (1) people are developed (through training, etc.) so they can perform better on the job; (2) jobs are used as the vehicle for developing people, professionally and personally (designing jobs around people, for example). Most organizations justify staff development based on the first rationale—more productivity—and ignore the latter.

At a time when managers bemoan the lack of loyalty among employees, the development of staff loyalty is a significant need. Increasingly, people have become more loyal to their profession than to their company: "I'm a software engineer" has replaced "I'm an IBM-er." Or they've become loyal only to themselves (if then). Underneath this trend, one can sense a deep longing for community. Does it have to be this way? I think not.

Especially for companies relying on "knowledge workers"—for example, in high-tech industries—issues like corporate loyalty, the use of a person's "discretionary time" for work, job design, staff recruitment, and work motivation all hinge on creating this two-way street.

This is truly a way to gain the highest levels of commitment from staff, and to retain people much longer than average for an industry. After all, who would want to leave a situation where they were continually growing? This two-way street includes the complement to the traditional model of staff training and development and has significant implications for job design: We must design jobs around the persons we work with, to help them reach their next stage of professional and personal development, rather than just trying to develop persons to fit into predefined jobs.

When that happens, you get the kind of reponses that Suzanne's team have given:

- *There's a very strong feeling of empowerment now. I know I don't need to wait 4 days to get permission to do something from management. I'm trusted for my experience to do my job and make the right call. I feel like I'm 30 to 40 percent more efficient.*

- *Over all, we're working more time under more pressure. And because of my team and my management, it's all been worth it.*

- *Before, we probably would have let customers complain and not done anything. Now we've opened ourselves up to our customers and asked how we could better meet their needs. We're trying to listen and respect them.*

- *On average I'm taking one-third less time to put out the same amount of work.*

- *It's amazing to me. Some days I'm doing 20 percent more, other days, I'm doing 100 percent more work. The change is in me, our team, and the work environment.*

- *We're crossing team lines and giving ideas on how to improve work flow, looking at different ways to do things. We've got a ways to go, but the willingness is there, and I see examples everyday.*

- *I can't put a price on how less anxious I feel.*

There are also implications for the mind-set of "Human Resources" and "Human Resource Development." When those terms were first introduced into corporate language, they appropriately replaced the more limited notion of "Personnel." It also sounded more like a business function, referring to "resource development." Yet that same feature is what makes it an outdated notion for Quantum Quality. It still implies that people can be managed in the same vein as other resources—land, material, financial, informational—are managed. It can imply, "Well we have 10 tons of steel and we have fifty bodies ("head count"). How do we put them all to work?"

Even worse is the notion of "Human Capital." Only on one level do people "invest" themselves, or are investments to be managed. To limit our thinking to that level depersonalizes the relationship, makes it a transaction instead of a communion. People are a more dynamic resource than these others, capable of shifting their value and controllability.

The two-way-street style of development begs for a newer label such as "associate development." "staff optimization," or . . . (any other ideas out there?).

The goal for both individuals and the companies they work for is the experience of growth, success, and the pursuit of happiness. We're all seeking to be happy, to be fulfilled, to be successful. So, what is success?

Any definition of success requires a wholistic view of who we are and what we're doing on this earth. Success is much more than making money, getting a promotion, more than that silly notion of "whoever dies with the most toys wins" (cars, homes, jewelry, techogadgets, countries visited, whatever). Success is a combination of both inner fulfillment and outer achievement.

As inner fulfillment, it's a sense of well-being, purposefulness, harmony with oneself as well as with one's family, friends, and colleagues. Inner fulfillment is related to our spiritual, emotional, physical, and mental enrichment: developing our deepest personal values and character; opening ourselves to experience our full emotional spectrum; being willing to act on our deepest aspirations; sharpening our capacity for clear perception and insight.

As outer achievement, success is also making a difference, achieving important goals, using one's talents and experience to make a contribution to others (including customers and clients). Outer success is also related to our spiritual, emotional, physical, and mental levels: carrying out our "calling," our purpose in life and work; promoting harmony with others; empowering ourselves to persist in attaining our goals; responding creatively to life.

How *do* we bring those two halves together—the inner and outer forms of success? Someone who seems to have done this is Mary Nelson, president of Bethel New Life, a community-development corporation in West Side Chicago. Mary first arrived there to help her brother get settled in as a new pastor—and she faced a problem right away.

> *Four days after we arrived there was the first riot. The community was up in flames and people were killed. It was obvious that traditional things weren't going to work. So we had to begin to do whatever needed to be done, and it was a matter of rolling up our sleeves and figuring out how are we going to tackle these problems. We gathered a group of people from the streets who were hurting, really hurting inside, to say, "How do we turn this hurt into figuring out what little steps we could take?" It was like being thrown into the fire.*
>
> *I started out with the very practical concern that there were so many houses being torn down. If we didn't do something about housing, there wouldn't be a community left. Between 1970 and 1980 we lost over 200 housing units per year in a square mile area.*
>
> *The church was a congregation of poor people. About 1/3 was on welfare or some kind of fixed income. We wanted to create a low-income housing alternative to the welfare system. A group of us got together and said, "Here is what we want to do in place of what is obviously not working." We went to the governor's office and all of the bureaucrats sat there and said, "You can't do that because of this and this and this. . . ." And we said, "Forget all the reasons why you can't do things and let's just do it."*

Mary and the congregation had to dig deep inside for courage and energy, and to search outside for the knowledge they needed to focus on realistic goals.

> *People said, "We've got to do it, because this is going to be a visible symbol, a visible statement that the church cares, that this is our community." As Martin Luther King Jr. said, "We know finite disappointment, but we know infinite hope." We know how the story ends. We have the sense that what we*

do, with God's help, makes a difference. It may not be in our lifetime, but there is hope and there are possibilities. I think that without hope, it doesn't happen.

One solution was "sweat equity," where people invest their own labor to fix up an apartment building in return for a share of the ownership. Even that took capital.

We mortgaged the church building five times. That was something that we loved and cared for, so we were putting up "earnest money." That was really earnest value that we were sticking into the project. It gave (the bankers) comfort that we were going to do everything in our power so that this project would not go belly-up.

For Mary, success came in many forms.

We had some learning experiences, some offshoots of the process. It not only makes affordable housing available to people who didn't have any cash, but it's a great leadership development tool. People who never thought they could lead people, that anyone would ever listen to what they had to say, would find out that they were leaders—that they had skills they never knew they had. And it changes the mentality from a tenant to a homeowner. People find out that "This is our building, and we got to see that repairs are done, and we have to get on each other's cases."

It also is a wonderful "can-do" experience that carries over into other things. A nice thing about a building is that it is so visible. You can stand back and say, "Man, look what we did. Doesn't this look great?" It's a positive accomplishment that bolsters everyone's self-image and "can-do" spirit. So when it comes to the drug pusher down the street, they're not so cowed. They say, "Wow, we did this building, then why can't we get rid of that drug pusher? We can do it."

To me, that's what gives Mary more than just a job. She's found a way to invest her deepest values in her work. The journey of her work, and our own, is truly a twofold one. Each problem we face, each challenge we take on at work, can be an opportunity—first, to make a creative difference in the world; second, to deepen our knowledge of who we are and what we're about.

And when we develop our inner resources and values, we gain the confidence to get ourselves and others out of the labyrinth of old, unworkable patterns. Then, we can take the best of who we are and make a rich contribution to our colleagues, our customers, and our community. In this twofold way, our work can even become heroic.

Frank Carrubba's study of excellence in HP Labs showed the balance of inner and outer success while defining the differing roles of leaders and managers.

> *The magic, the chemistry, I think, in any good project is having a good balance between leadership and management. Building spirit among people goes beyond just the individuals and their immediate peers. It is a bonding those groups have in spirit to other groups, as well as to some overlying purpose.*
>
> *Good business decisions have to go along with good research. Inspiration on the part of the leader has to be balanced with good management practices.*
>
> *A leader is someone who inspires, who is the stimulator, behind a project that people are willing to commit to, people are willing to go that one extra step for. The opportunity is, the excitement is, to be among those who have changed the course of the world in some small way, or in some major way. "Management is taking care of your responsibility to the people in terms of salary, environment, benefits, tools, and support that they need to do their job and to be the best that they can be."*

Therefore, understanding how to apply our values in our work is a critical step to unleashing the power of innovation, quality, and customer satisfaction.

Strengthening the System

For the Focus stage, there are four new factors for developing "systems integrity" for QQ. In this chapter, innovation is based on the principle of making employee development a two-way street. Managers and team leaders can empower teams for QQ by aligning the teams on the factors of: Group Values and Talent Base. In the next chapter, continuous improvement is based on looking at issues from a "systems" perspective. Managers and team leaders can empower teams for QQ by aligning the teams on the factors of Communication Structure, and Information Management.

One key factor for empowering quality teams at this stage is aligning personal and group values with the organization's values (each impacting the other). The other is to develop the talent base through hiring, training, and other methods.

E. *Group Values.* This is the degree to which the team has a set of group values—"what we stand for"—that is compatible with the sponsors' values. When this is done well, the team has a defined set of values— "what we stand for"—that is closely aligned with their sponsor's values; the sponsors actively practice values such as risk taking, openness, trust, and respect, and the team actively practices those same values.

F. *Talent Base.* This is the degree to which the team has the necessary talent and experience it needs to achieve its goals. When this is done well, the team has obtained the range of talent it needs, has resources needed for training and development; sponsors have provided a system for technical as well as management development linked with annual career-development planning.

As sponsors and teams align on these two issues, they will foster a culture in which they work to develop the talent and spirit in themselves and each other to be all they can be. Skill banks, values certification, and team building are some of the tools that can help institutionalize this aspect of a positive sponsor-team relationship.

Practicing the Paradigm

Learning

The key question that stimulates and organizes learning in the Focus stage is "What's empowering?" When we continually ask, answer, and reask that question, it will lead us to learn what we need in order to:

(E) develop internal confidence and fortitude
(F) identify and develop the needed levels of knowledge and skills

The level of learning found in a learning organization depends on empowered individuals and teams. This empowerment, in turn, is sustained by the way people at all levels in the organization encourage the development of this confidence and talent up, down, and across—in their managers, subordinates, and peers. Indeed, to make the move to an empowered, learning organization, as managers move into the role of "servants to those they've empowered," subordinates must move into the role of building the confidence of those managers who have the courage to "let go" and to deliberately bolster the talent base of the manager through their own development.

The more introspective type of inquiry is also needed for this to happen. We can ask ourselves, "Where do I draw my confidence from: my talent, my values, my spirituality, or what?" Or, "What are the knowledge and skills I can bring to work with which I can make a difference?" From the answers to these and similar questions, we can empower ourselves as no one else can. Then, we can feel, "We're confident and empowered!"

Values

There is a level of confidence and empowerment that no other person, and no circumstances, can give us. We have to draw it from within ourselves. We all have deep reserves of energy, determination, caring—but it is as though we have covered these reserves over with years of frustration or neglect, so that we no longer may believe they're in us.

We have to search within ourselves, and in others, to find who we truly are—as whole human beings, not as fragmented products of our decisions based on growing up and living in an unhealthy society. We have to be fierce in labeling what is only superficially ourself or selves and what is our essence: the truth of who we really are and who we really can become.

And, then, we must take it the next level: to act according to what we find in ourselves. This brings about a state of integrity, where what we think, what we say, and what we do are congruent and aligned.

This truth seeking about our own identity and magnificence can be scary. We may have to stretch ourselves to fulfill the potential we see. Yet not to stretch, not to grow our healthy selves, is to live in quiet despair a life that was never its own.

This truth seeking about the potential in others also demands of us—as leaders, managers, employees—a commitment to evoking the best in each other. The Latin word *educare* literally means "to lead out from, to lead forth." Our derived word *education* originally meant "to bring out the wisdom and deepest truths from a person," not to pour it into an empty vessel. We must switch from an emphasis on teaching others to an emphasis on facilitating others' learning as well as our own.

Creativity

Developing both the talent base and the personal motivation in making staff development a two-way street can make an enormous contribution to the quality of ideas generated at each stage of the Creative Journey. The focus for creativity at this first step of the Focus Stage is *inner* develop-ment—strengthening one's character, confidence, values, persistence, and moral fiber. This inner development often happens naturally when we recognize that, because we are all part of a vast creation, we share in its creative nature. We take our own creative urges as natural, important, life-giving to others and ourselves. This development can also be pursued more deliberately through personal growth experiences, conscious net-working with people we can communicate with openly about wants, fears, and so on. Overall, growing our creative talents happens rather "seasonally"—spurts of growth and periods of dormancy emerge that simply ask for time of us the insights to gel.

Sustainability

The word "wealth" comes from "weal," which draws on the same root as the words "whole" and "health." Sustainability requires a *conscious con-centration on wealth, health, and wholeness as inseparable aspects* of the qual-ity of life, much like multiple facets of a single diamond. True wealth exists only when the companies, people, and society as a whole are healthy—which is not the case today. Symptoms of an unhealthy econ-omy, such as huge budget deficits, have root causes in the unhealthy deci-sions we've made based on selfish rather than holistic thinking.

It is interesting to ask about how one's personal lifestyle might be reflected in business decisions. Are those who take make choices for the optimum health and sustainability of their bodies also the ones who are more likely to make business decisions for the optimum health of the environment and society? Are those who abuse their bodies, through poor diet, stress, etc., also more likely to abuse the earth with their busi-ness choices? Although I don't know the answers to these questions for sure, we *are* generally prone to carrying one pattern of thought and behavior over into other parts of our lives. And our consciousness of good health, added to an awareness of wholeness, is a key to the production of true wealth.

Living this two-way street, making a difference in the world, becom-ing all we can be. . . . If we could bring our deepest values to the task, find an inner meaning to what we're doing, see work as a heartfelt exercise of our souls rather than as a mere job we "have to do," then our work and our lives much the wealthier.

7

Analyze Issues from a "Systems" Perspective

As a business, we use the Baldridge criteria as a world class criteria to benchmark against, using an internal assessment process two years in a row. And it not only gives the normal benchmark score, but also helps us to focus on the systems that need to be fixed.

—Bob Vogenthaler, total quality manager, Procter & Gamble's Health Care Division

Mastering the Mind-Set

In the second stage of the QQ process, the Focus Stage, we begin working on the Challenge in two steps: tapping into our character (to gain confidence in meeting the challenge) and analyzing the key issues and priorities for improvement. As shown in Figure 7.1, in this chapter, we'll address the second step for deepening our understanding of a challenge in a Quantum Quality way: Analyzing issues from a "systems" perspective.

For Bob Vogenthaler, improving the culture for quality is not an end in itself:

Our internal Baldridge assessment workhelps uncover the systems and reinforces thinking around the Plan–Do–Check–Act cycle. Using the feedback, we want to know what areas we can focus on that would (1) move us toward Baldridge-winning performance levels and (2) also have the highest probability of impacting business results.

By doing an appropriate analysis, we can define the objectives and goals for the organization that are breakthrough in nature. Then we ask, "How are you going to go about achieving those objectives and goals through the

4. THE
COMPLETION

1. THE
CHALLENGE

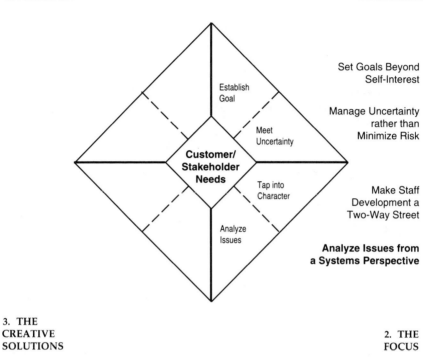

3. THE
CREATIVE
SOLUTIONS

2. THE
FOCUS

FIGURE 7.1. The Creative Journey™

strategies and measures that we select?" Those strategies ought to be break-through-focused as well.

Some of the key systems Bob's division at P&G focused on after the first internal assessment were: strategy development, product launch, and customer relations. They hoped these would be leverage points for enhancing the overall culture and performance of the organization through strategic initiatives.

In the area of strategy development and deployment, it got us to make a conscious decision to adopt a particular planning model that's being used in our company. It's [a matter of] getting clear on the choices for elevating a specific element or two of the business to breakthrough, and then focusing strategies and resources against that breakthrough area.

The focus on product launch meant aligning the organization on the right choices for what we work on, communicating those choices to the orga-

nization, and then executing these initiatives in the marketplace. They were choices related to product quality and people capabilities. Now it's a matter of getting it deployed more profitably.

In our consumer relations area, we have an 800 line for contact with consumers. To elevate the importance of the service we provide, we aimed at raising the response rate and the degree of satisfaction with the contact. A year ago our contact with consumers—the first time they call in—was less than 50 percent; the rest of them would either wait for a long period of time or hang up and have to call back. Driving that, today we're at about 75 percent and wanting to get that into the mid-90s.

In this focus on customers, Procter & Gamble has been trying to do more than just improve the degree of satisfaction:

One of the vision pieces that has been adopted by this business is the concept of consumer delight. We tie it back to a model from Dr. [Noriaki] Kano in Japan. There's really three types of performance that you can give a consumer. One is just meeting the basic needs. And all it does is it gets you in the game. If you don't deliver against that, it's a dissatisfier action. In the example of toothpaste, it's a product that lathers and cleans your teeth well and provides cavity protection. All products do that today.

The second would be performance—things like tartar control, adding new benefits. The better you deliver against those benefits, the higher the satisfaction you deliver to consumers.

The third are these unexpected benefits. Consumers don't expect it, so not having it there is not a dissatisfier, but having it there causes some excitement that goes beyond satisfaction, to delight and gets you a more loyal consumer. In the toothpaste business that could be the "neat squeeze" package, a new package we have out on the market, with some unique things that take it well beyond the tube.

The initiatives on strategy development, product launch, and customer relations addressed only a small subset of the twenty-eight examination items of the Baldrige criteria. What was the impact of finding creative ways to improve these systems?

When we came back the second year and did an assessment, the overall score went up 5 percent, but the areas we chose to focus on went up 50 percent— up dramatically from a score standpoint. Business results year to year have made excellent growth, we believe partly attributable to the quality initiative work. There are other factors, but believe me, this is one of them.

If you were in a sales department and your best product began a decline in sales, what would you do? Develop a new sales promotion? Ask people in the new product pipeline when the newer products would be available? Bring together a team from all departments—perhaps to include R&D, engineering, manufacturing, operations, purchasing, marketing, finance, and sales—and examine possible causes? If you did the latter, how would you deal with the potential defensiveness of the departments, each (including sales) not wanting to be blamed for the decline?

In other words, when is a problem solely your own and when is it a more complex, systemic issue?

The need for quality improvement often comes when top management develops a new strategy for operating in the marketplace. Yet, a new strategy is worthless unless people in an organization *understand the "systems" complexity of doing what's necessary* to find a solution and implement it, thereby producing innovations in products, services, delivery, and operating practices.

Because the parts of our organizations are integral to the whole, we can understand the parts only by seeing the pattern of the whole. This is the "systemic" game of understanding parts and wholes, where we might make our most significant discoveries that lead us to a targeted innovation.

A system is a structure that supersedes and gives meaning to what the mind would call "constituent parts." This structure will hold a certain amount of oscillation and energy without shifting; this makes for stability in life. The way a system changes—and this includes psychological structures of an individual as well as even biological systems—is like the way water turns to steam when it's 212°F (100°C): The molecules remain as water (i.e., they hold the structure and energy) until the point when they become a gas. That is, the structure breaks and makes a quantum jump to reformulate itself into a new structure, which then will remain stable until a second, higher threshold is crossed.

A systems analysis is most helpful to understand the strategy and leverage points for introducing enough energy to reformulate the system. To see what a systemic analysis entails, consider the following example.

For one nationwide health insurance carrier, the competitive marketplace virtually dictated the need for a new, computerized claims-processing system. The company developed one that could process almost 90 percent of the claims automatically, twice the effectiveness of the older system. But the company found its implementation failing. The transition was complicated because the claims-processing jobs were so different.

Good performance using the previous computer system was not necessarily adequate qualification for the new jobs.

Most employees attended a formal five-week training program to work on the new system. Special tests were used to determine who would likely succeed in the new jobs. Employees became agitated because if they didn't pass the formal classroom training, they stood not to be returned to their old job—or any job (because the old system was being phased out). Loyal service and good productivity weren't being acknowledged. The "you bet your job" contract also introduced enormous pressure on the final exams.

As a result, turnover during and after the formal training periods was double the normal rate. The entire employee-development process was reevaluated, including recruitment, pretesting, selection, on-the-job training, and on-the-job support. The feasibility of implementing the computer system, the work-measurement, and the quality-assurance programs were also being reevaluated.

Defining the problem systematically was the first issue. Defining it strictly as a "morale" problem, a "turnover" problem, a "training" problem, a "computer system" problem, or a "quality assurance" problem would have led only to partial solutions. Supervisors, trainers, recruiters, computer systems people—were all making decisions that made sense given the pressures they individually were under. The result was a "catch-22" reaction: The more they did to correct the problems they individually encountered, the more something else in the system undercut the potential benefits.

For example, the classroom and on-the-job training process failed to meet production demands. As shown by the systems flowchart of Figure 7.2, the need to increase productivity led to scheduling more trainees and more classes per time period. Trainers had fewer days between courses to prepare and update materials. Given their lack of on-the-job experience and the updates on the new system, their class examples were not always current. There was a greater need for on-the-job training to bring trainees up to full productivity. But because the on-the-job trainers (the technical specialists) were also working on production backlogs, they had less time to give. So, more trainees ended up not performing at the level necessary to impact the backlogs.

Each separate group in this process made understandable decisions given the pressures they were under. Their separate "solutions" compounded the problem rather than solving it. The problem lay in the system of interactions.

By exploring these and three other paradoxes' the following analogy for change emerged, (see Figure 7.3).

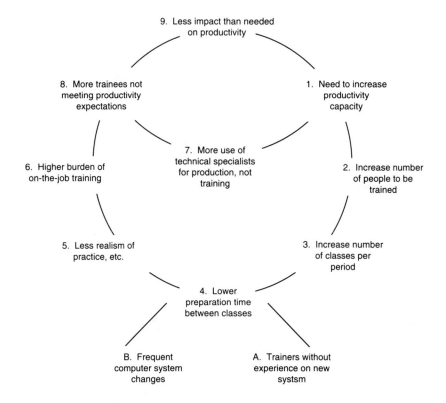

FIGURE 7.2.   Systems Analysis of a Trainee/Productivity Issue

SOURCE: *The Creative Edge,* © 1987 by William C. Miller. Reprinted with permission of Addison-Wesley Publishing Company, Inc.

If we aim for port 2 and land there, it is very difficult to also land at port 1! If quality-assurance programs, for example, have the primary purpose of measuring productivity and supporting disciplinary actions, it will be difficult to use that program to improve quality. In other words, measuring performance is a key part of improving quality, but improving quality is not necessarily part of a program to measure performance. The actions of the insurance company were aimed at port 2 even though its stated destination was port 1.

The solution was not in changing any one thing, not even in a series of single changes.

What was needed to implement the innovative computer system was a "critical mass" of changes. This "package" needed to involve *leverage points* that would impact the system.

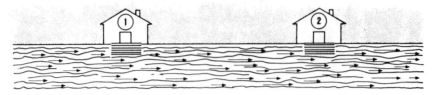

Imagine a fast flowing river with two landing ports and jungle in between:

Port #1 is:	Port #2 is:
"Enhance, build, improve quality"	Measures, assure, enforce quality"
"Build on positive employee motivations"	"Direct policies at hard-to-motivate employees"
"Develop high quality of trainees"	"Develop large quantity of trainees"

IF YOU TARGET PORT #2, IT IS VERY DIFFICULT TO GET BACK TO PORT #1.

FIGURE 7.3.   Strategic Targets

SOURCE: *The Creative Edge,* © 1987 by William C. Miller. Reprinted with permission of Addison-Wesley Publishing Company, Inc.

The final recommendations emphasized a landing at Port 1. Eighty proposed actions were grouped into: mandatory short- and long-term, optional short- and long-term. Each set of actions was designed to be implemented as a whole. Implementing a few items from each package might produce some short-term gains, but wouldn't deliver substantive change.

After reading this case, you might wonder, "What's the use? Can I help to accomplish any real change in my organization!" You might feel this especially if you're trying to change a cultural norm (for example, making the organization "more market-driven"). The paradox you face is this: although organizational change can be formidable, it is also within your influence when you can see your organization as a whole system and when you truly know your own power, love, and wisdom.

When different groups come together to look at a problem more systemically, the differences in power, perspective, and agenda can be hard to overcome. Perry Gehring (vice president of research for DowElanco) points out the cross-functional nature of doing business today:

Another thing that took a major tilt forward when we came here, was getting the commercial organization involved all the way back to discovery. Commercial business managers now are assigned to those basic research materials doing commercial evaluations. It wasn't so easy to get commercial folks enthusiastic about things that are six or seven years away. But, it's probably the single most important thing we did with respect to this process. And the reason is quite simple—I've said it's kind of like a relay race: If you run the first three laps of the mile relay and the fourth person isn't even on the track yet, you have a problem.

Without a respect for differences, systems analysis and change become impossible. When respect is hard to come by in a competitive situation—such as union versus management—how can one begin to bridge the gap? That was the challenge for Roger James, an organizational consultant who worked with a major utility.

What we have been doing here is working on several levels . . . to try and improve the relationship and alignment between the company and the employees and the unions who represent them. Just to get them to understand each other so they can solve their common problems together is a major undertaking.

Leading through service is the key. I honor both cultures that are being represented. Their success is what matters to me—their joint success. At first, the utility's supervisors thought I was trying to sell them something or trying to snow them. Of course they didn't want to have any part of that. The good news was that there was somebody in that group who was willing to raise that issue, give me the feedback, so I could deal with it.

Roger also had to create trust with the union members without compromising his own values and identity.

I wanted to learn everything about them, their culture, who they are and why the see what they see as valuable . . . learning as much as I possibly could about unions, the union movement, labor law, labor relations, to be able to talk knowledgeably about that, to honor that—to really say truthfully, "I understand it, I value it, and my role here is to make sure that the unions, the company, and the people who represent them remain whole."

Roger seems to represent an integration of meeting his clients needs and personal meaning from the work. That integration is based on his values of service and well-being. This is the practical level of taking on a challenge, investing it with one's values, and getting something to happen that serves others.

Yet even the best cross-functional team—complete with great talent, communications, vision, values, and such—can come up short in its work, depending on its relationship with the rest of the organization, particularly its sponsoring management. That is, there are a multitude of factors that affect the effectiveness of the QQ process beyond the cross-functional aspects of the organizational system.

As mentioned in Chapter Three, the author's research has shown that there are sixteen factors for developing a Quantum Quality culture. In each of the last few chapters, we have reviewed two factors for "Strengthening the System" at each step of the Creative Journey; the full process of eight steps entails sixteen factors (practices and behavior) for management to negotiate with teams.

Creating the environment for sustainable growth—for the organization, the people, and the society—depends on managing the entire Creative Journey. We've already reviewed the factors of: Purpose/Vision, Roles/Authority, Business/Technology Environment, Key Success Factors, Group Values, and Talent Base. The others are shown in Figure 7.4 and will be described as this book progresses.

Team leaders and members can negotiate stronger support during each stage of their QQ journey by knowing which factors are most important for the stage they're at. Executives and managers can strategize how to develop the "systems integrity" for supporting all the teams reporting to them—making sure that the system does what they believe and say needs to happen. This model helps everyone manage the complex of practices and tools that it takes to add the dimensions of *learning, values, creativity, and sustainability* to the QC/QA and TQM dimensions of inspection, measurement of results, statistical analysis, process improvement, empowerment, teamwork, customer focus, and speed.

Performance on the sixteen factors for fostering a QQ culture can be measured and graphically displayed (see Figure 7.5). In Figure 7.5, a high score on a specific factor indicates high alignment and linkage between a team and its sponsoring management. Look for factors where further dialogue between team and sponsor can improve the linkage. When a team and its sponsors' scores are given below, identify leverage points for improvement by looking for (1) agreement regarding low scores; (2) agreement regarding high scores; (3) different opinions about scores (gaps); and (4) historical momentum of improvement (if available).

In this case, there is high alignment between the sponsors and team leaders for work in the two early stages of the Quantum Quality process—the Challenge and the Focus. However, the "systems integrity" breaks down in the final two stages—the Creative Solution and the Completion. This is symptomatic of "early empowerment" cultures that get teams launched in the right direction but fail to provide the full systems support for "follow through" and ultimate success.

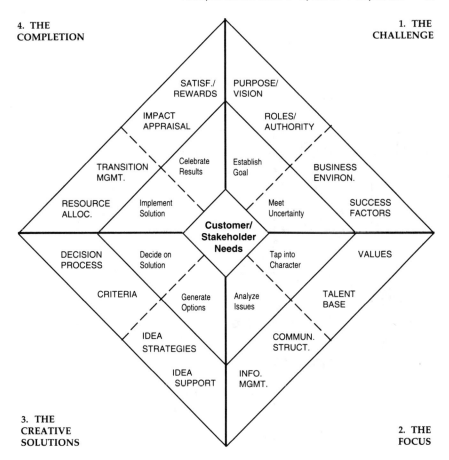

FIGURE 7.4.   Strategic Innovation Management™

William Grundstrom, formerly of Motorola and a senior vice president of the American Productivity and Quality Center in Houston, once said that the quality movement was strong on tools and techniques and strong on measuring quality, as with the Baldrige criteria. However, he added, there's a weakness in modeling which management practices and culture can best be implemented to utilize the tools and meet the criteria throughout the organization. He saw SIMAP as the most significant development in this area, providing, as it does, a holistic road map for a focused implementation. It also develops a common language and framework (or a reference point) from which to monitor the organization's progress. In fact, the Baldrige criteria can be linked to SIMAP factors (see Table 7.1).

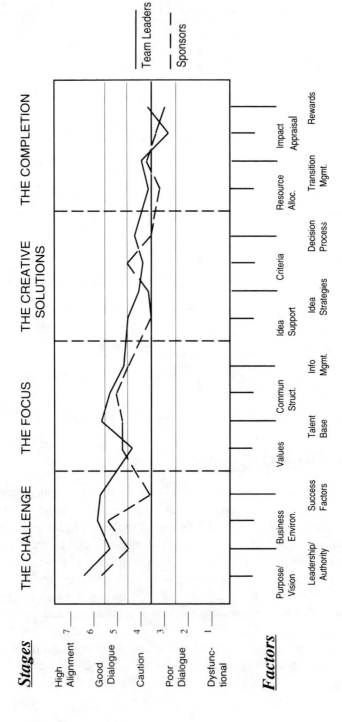

FIGURE 7.5. Strategic Innovation Management™ Assessment Profile (SIMAP®)

SOURCE: *The Creative Edge*, © 1987 by William C. Miller. Reprinted with permission of Addison-Wesley Publishing Company, Inc.

TABLE 7.1.

Baldrige Criteria (% Importance)	SIMAP Factors
Leadership (9.5%)	Purpose/Vision
	Roles/Authority
Strategic Quality Planning (6%)	Business/Tech Environment
	Key Success Factors
Human Resource Development	Group Values
and Management (15%)	Talent Base
Information and Analysis (7.5%)	Commun. Structure
	Information Management
Management of Process Quality (14%)	Team Idea Support
	Idea-Generating Strategies
	Criteria
	Decision Process
Quality and Operational Results (18%)	Resource Allocation
	Transition Management
	Impact Appraisal
	Satisfaction/Rewards
Customer Focus and Satisfaction (30%)	Purpose/Vision
	Key Success Factors
	Impact Appraisal
	Satisfaction/Rewards
	(Other Factors also)

The wave of the future is the organization that is totally fluid, totally flexible, totally focused on the end results (both achievement and learning). To create, to anticipate, or even to cope with this current of change, we cannot simply legislate that it happen. We have to roll up our sleeves and get involved in *making* change, and fully expect that we may not even see the final outcome of the work that we do. Until we're willing to do that, there can be no constructive change.

This totally fluid organization depends on continuous learning and improvement, both leaping changes and incremental. As Chris Ehlers, transportation operations manager for Procter & Gamble, tells us:

> *It requires us to constantly be reevaluating the organization as an entity, and to set the organization up to be flexible. To change the work system in trans-portation services, we originally did a very hierarchical, socio-technical*

design with skill levels. A year after we put it in, we scrapped it. The members of the organization came up with what they call a "fluid focus system" where they're constantly reevaluating the processes and what the needs are.

Chris's colleagues set up the organization so that there were people with the multiple skills needed to actually do the work. As needs in the organization arise over the short term, people came together around the need, handled it, and then retracted from it.

For instance, one focus was contract management. We had about fifteen hundred carriers nationwide, each of whose contracts had point-to-point rates for within the United States rather than tariffs. That meant millions of rates in the computer system. Well, we had one very cold winter and fuel prices went through the roof. Our carriers' profit margins were not great. So they came to us and requested a 6 percent increase to cover these higher fuel costs. They made a case and we agreed.

We took one look at our computer system and realized we'd have to change each of the rates individually. Yet there were only three people with responsibility for managing contracts. We fell back on the fluid system we had created. Everybody just stopped what they were doing, collapsed around the contract piece until the rates were changed. Full time, two weeks. They then turned to the systems people who were also helping them with the rates and said, "You know we need to change this." They said, "No sweat. While we were making all these rate changes, we figured out what to do." They put in a program so we could make one change to change all the rates in the system.

Getting that to happen throughout an organization is challenging. Systems analysis can be a vehicle for changing the way managers conduct their role in the organization, as Bob Vogenthaler of Procter & Gamble points out:

One of the powers of using the internal assessment process is that it leads to learning on the part of the leadership team and commitment building. They learned by doing it.

The key thing that we're learning about is the role of the immediate manager, and the linkage between the immediate manager and their subordinate. We're thinking about splitting out some work for breakthrough activity in the immediate manager's role. It's not in performance reviews, career development discussions, or the more traditional personnel administration. It's how well is the immediate manager relationship doing in aligning and communicating what the choices are, in helping involve people at all levels in the organization to the choices that are being made.

Strengthening the System

In addition to the factors outlined in the previous chapter—Group Values and Talent Base—managers and team leaders can empower teams in the Focus stage by aligning the teams on the factors of Communication Structure and Information Management—all with the aim of enhancing the ability to analyze issues from a systems perspective.

The first key to empowering quality teams at this stage is developing communication structures that align with and yet supersede decision-making structures. The second is managing the information flow to provide open, targeted, "just-in-time" data to quality teams.

G. *Communication Structure.* This is the degree to which the team has access to everyone inside and outside the organization who can help it define and understand its problem better. When this is done well, the team communicates easily with people in other functions, keeps all sponsors and team members up to date on progress; the sponsors make effective use of committees and task forces to resolve issues that cut across more than one project team.

H. *Information Management.* This is the degree to which the team has access to the most critical information it needs to analyze the key issues. When this is done well, the team has open access to all information it needs to analyze key issues, uses specific data-collection and analysis tools, has computer capabilities for rapid digestion of data, and analyzes issues from a "systems" perspective.

As sponsors and teams align on these two issues, they will foster a culture in which they process and share information precisely and openly, quality function deployment, capability assessments, and systems/network diagrams are some of the tools that can help institutionalize this aspect of a positive sponsor-team relationship.

Practicing the Paradigm

Learning

As we've seen, the key question that stimulates and organizes learning in the Focus stage is, "What's empowering?," which includes not only

"What gives us confidence to take on this challenge?," but also "What are the key issues and priorities to concentrate on?"

Chapter Six stated that in asking "What gives us confidence?", we must learn how to

(E) develop internal confidence and fortitude

(F) identify and develop the needed levels of knowledge and skills

For the question "What are the key issues and priorities?" we must learn how to

(G) create diverse, broad-based teams and networks for working together (cross-functionally, cross-organizationally, etc.) without unnecessary centralization of control

(H) gathering and distributing information for systemic analysis of key issues

A learning organization must break down the "silos"—the barriers sealing in functional specialties—to allow learning and innovation to occur at the interfaces between them. This indeed is where most of the breakthroughs will occur, even in scientific disciplines.[1] This means finding solutions to overcome barriers, ranging from "Our offices aren't close enough for easy communication" to "Our budgets will be cut if we use people from other departments for this rather than our own."

This cross-functional communication is useful only to the extent that the shared information is broad enough and packaged well enough (in understandable reports, etc.). Only then can we convert a collection of individual learners into a true learning community.

Self-inquiry is also important for opening up these channels. If we ask, "How do I try to control information and communication for the sake of managing and/or sharing power?" or "How do I work to break down prejudices between various groups?" we can empower others as well as ourselves. Then we can feel, "We welcome diverse viewpoints!"

Values

To understand the whole truth about what's operating in a situation, truthful communications, openness, authenticity, and respect for diver-

---

[1] For example, the VCR could not be invented until six different technology streams could be brought together—which couldn't occur without each stream's maturation and the cross-discipline exploration to find their linkages and symbiotic capabilities.

sity are essential. Developing this truthfulness allows for the unfolding of all the talent a team brings to solving a challenge; without it, the talent lies wasted like last year's grain harvest sitting unused in a silo.

Given, this last analogy, it is no accident (perhaps) that when we separate organizational functions, such as marketing and engineering, we refer to them as "silos." Truthful understanding, across functions, requires truthful communications. Ultimately, only in knowing the whole truth, seeing the unity within the diversity and multiplicity of events, can creativity be fostered. Only when Gorbachev stood up in the Soviet Parliament and stated, "The communist system isn't working" could the energy be freed up to find creative alternatives. Hiding the truth takes so much energy that nothing new can be born.

Creativity

Creativity that isn't focused on the right issue at the right time is usually wasted energy (except for the accidental discoveries that are more serendipitous than planned).

TQM offers a great many analytical tools and methodologies. These tools identify the key leverage points for improvement and provide a clear focus for subsequent creative thinking.

Developing, selecting, or adapting the right tool for the right situation is more than a rote exercise; and adapting tools to unique situations can require a great deal of creativity. Last but not least, creative juices tend to get going when the right mix begins to communicate well. Bringing diverse people together and getting them to work synergetically can be the greatest creative challenge of all.

Sustainability

Knowing the whole truth demands that we *seek the wisdom of a systems perspective*, a global view, when we investigate the causes and effects that our thoughts, words, and deeds might have on others and the environment. Operating from the viewpoint of "we're one system, not isolated components" evokes a more inclusive and therefore truthful analysis. Only with this level of full appreciation for the consequences of our actions can we make intelligent decisions. And intelligent decisions, with this perspective, will be more compassionate because of this inclusive perspective.

A systems perspectives also points out the fallacy of our overemphasis on competition—both within a company and with others in an industry. The movement toward strategic alliances between "competitors"—as found more and more in the automobile, electronics, pharmaceutical, and biotechnology industries—is evidence of waking up to the *need* for focusing on serving customer needs rather than killing the competition. Bob Vogenthaler of P&G sees this as a necessary, but difficult, transition we need to make.

> *Unfortunately, the habit of win–win is not readily adopted by a lot of American industries. It would pay off, but I think our competitive culture gets in the way. It's just the current paradigm—organizations believe you've got to have competition and win against it.*
>
> *It would be better to say, "Let's focus on the breakthrough choices we must make just to increase value for and delight our consumer. And it's all right if our competition does it, too. We can make the pie bigger, as Stephen Covey would say, rather than slicing it up.[2] Our activities are focused in winning in the marketplace by delivering more value."*

---

[2] See Stephen R. Covey, *The Seven Habits of Highly Effective People* (New York: Simon & Schuster, 1990).

8

Use Four Distinct Strategies to Find Creative Options

We were asked to do the impossible. We had a challenging business situation and some of our products were stymied in the marketplace. So we got the challenge to set up a system that would make a paradigm shift in coming up with a new product.

—Bill Diana, senior engineer, Exxon Chemical

Mastering the Mind-Set

In the third stage of the Creative Journey, we generate the Creative Solutions in two steps: finding the options and choosing the best one As shown in Figure 8.1, in this chapter we'll address the principle for achieving this goal in a Quantum Quality way: Using four distinct strategies to find creative options.

Faced with the challenge of developing a breakthrough product, Jon Stanet, technical project manager for this Exxon breakthrough team, had to pull together high-level expertise from many parts of the research organization. The initial task was to build a strong team out of this diverse group, some of whom would be core and some peripheral contributors.

Bill Diana was part of that core team:

We integrated the team-building skills that we developed earlier, emphasizing new ways of approaching problems and taking risks. We built high-performance teams based on a partnership with people in other divisions: Individuals were actually made a part of the team in name even though they were getting paid from a different product line. All team members had iden-

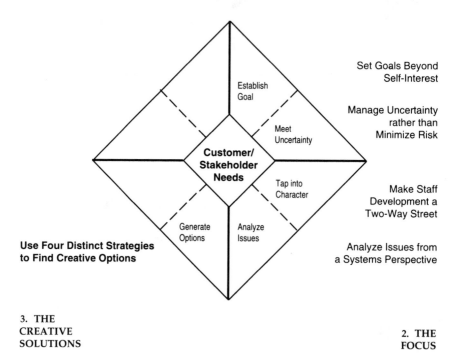

**4. THE
COMPLETION**

**1. THE
CHALLENGE**

Set Goals Beyond
Self-Interest

Manage Uncertainty
rather than
Minimize Risk

Make Staff
Development a
Two-Way Street

**Use Four Distinct Strategies
to Find Creative Options**

Analyze Issues from
a Systems Perspective

**3. THE
CREATIVE
SOLUTIONS**

**2. THE
FOCUS**

FIGURE 8.1.   The Creative Journey™

*tification with the primary task at hand, and we incorporated those individu-
als in every one of our brainstorming sessions.*

To begin the search for a creative solution, the team had to apply new
techniques. Rather than jumping to work in the laboratory, the usual
approach,

> *We did a lot of visioning techniques on paper before we put anything in a test
> tube. We looked at hundreds of chemistries to make a new product. We
> explored questions like, "How would we do the process development? How
> would we design this plant? What would be the environmental impact?" We
> narrowed it down to maybe a dozen possibilities.*
>
> *And when we started doing experimental work, we narrowed it down to
> four. Two looked like a sure thing, one was difficult. And the fourth looked
> like it could never be done, because the raw materials weren't even available
> and the chemistry was not even in the literature. Because one of our goals was*

to try to come up with stuff that was extremely proprietary, management supported it even though there was really a low probability that we'd ever make it.

We ran those experiments and ran into a blank wall. But we didn't quit: "It's got to be there." So we ended up inventing our own catalyst and our own raw material. We put it all together and it looked unbelievable.

But developing the chemistry was only the first hurdle to overcome. Although it might work fine in the labs, could the company upscale it to commercial production with the right economics attached to it?

We went to top management a year ago and said that we've got the chemistry, but we don't know how to make it commercially because we've got a lot of hurdles. Honest communication. We didn't sell them. We said this is the challenge. They looked at us and asked if we can do it; and we said we don't know how, but we'll commit that we're going to do it.

Now we're number two on the list. And we're vying for commercial equipment to get it out on time. We've got something that could be worth a lot in profit.

The product is still in the prove-it stage, but there has been sufficient success to begin to examine the lessons learned in achieving the leap in technology.

So teamwork, empowerment, making that leap, not being afraid, not being conservative, not backing off when you hit the wall—they've been key to developing this breakthrough technology.

What does it take to bring together a diverse group of people and (1) get everyone to work synergistically to generate possible creative solutions, while (2) not getting caught in a "creative group think" where everyone is brainstorming down the same path?

Imagine for a moment that you're the new manager of a production department (or marketing department) that has serious productivity and quality problems. Your company has made a major commitment to "Total Quality": to improve work processes and thus improve work outputs. You have been brought in to "transform" the department. As people talk to you about the department, you hear four categories of thought on the matter:

Group 1 says: "Things aren't really that bad. Sure, some things need improving, but basically the way we do things is sound. We don't need an overhaul, just small improvements that build on what we already do."

Group 2 says: "This department needs a major overhaul. The attitudes, the technologies, the work systems—they're all out of step with where we know we need to be five years from now. Let's set some clearheaded goals and do what it takes to achieve them."

Group 3 says: "To be frank, this place sure needs help to make it a more tolerable place. We need to get everyone involved in troubleshooting some obvious problems, and then develop some pilot programs. Let's try out a few new ideas and then we'll find out what else we need to work on."

And, finally, Group 4 says: "It's frustrating not being able to develop what we know are possibilities. We hope you let us leap out to the leading edge of what's possible, to go where no company has yet even dreamed of."

How would you go about bringing people together with these different perspectives? Those who see the need for more than incremental change may not "buy into" a process using statistical techniques to find current quality problems. Even brainstorming sessions could result in lots of storms with little brain power working toward common solutions.

Continuous, long-term improvement requires both *incremental and breakthrough improvements*. The model of Innovation Styles gives you four distinct strategies for QQ, generating options for both leaping and incremental improvements. Stimulated in part by the Values and Lifestyles Program at SRI International, research from Professor Michael Kirton of Hatfield Polytechnic (England), and the Myers–Briggs Type Indicator (MBTI), there are four fundamentally different ways that people approach innovation and change in their lives:

- The Visioning style: "Let's develop a clear sense of long-term purpose and goals to focus and drive our innovation efforts." People who emphasize the Visioning style in TQ programs can support innovation by providing "the big picture" and longer-term direction.

- The Modifying style: "Let's build on what we already have and make improvements where we can." People who emphasize the Modifying style in TQ programs can support innovation by being responsive to immediate needs and can maximize available resources to help the short-term motivation of groups by finding practical ways of getting immediate "successes."

- The Experimenting style: "Let's combine and test ideas systematically and learn from the results . . . and involve people to ensure an implementable action plan." People who emphasize the Experimenting style in TQ programs can support innovation by providing methods/systems to take risk in stages (with a good research design, for example) even when the outcome is uncertain and can make an idea implementable by getting people collaboratively involved in the decision making.

- The Exploring style: "Let's question our assumptions and explore to see where we end up, even though we have no clear goal in sight or methods to stick with." People who emphasize the Exploring style in TQ programs can support innovation by providing challenge to accepted ways of seeing things and seeking out novel approaches to problems.

As shown in Figure 8.2, these strategies are similar to approaching a challenge from any of four directions (north, west, south, east).

Each style is like a language. We each may have one or two "mother tongues," yet we can learn to "speak" and use all four change strategies. The Exploring style has often been stereotyped as the "creative" one. However, research from this author strongly suggests that people with

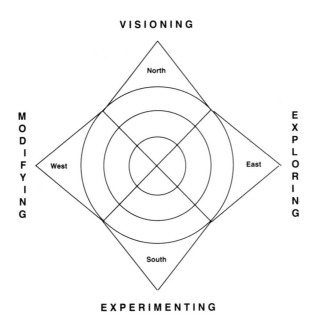

FIGURE 8.2.   Innovation Styles®

very different style patterns might be *equally* creative and each individual and each organization will employ a *mixture of all four styles*.[1]

Both of these notions—the potential for equal creativity, and the mixture of all four styles—hold a key for building commitment to and participation in QQ. These different approaches to handling a creative challenge are an important type of diversity found within teams and between teams and their sponsoring management. Although the balance of styles may vary somewhat situationally, we can find important patterns of dominant styles in groups and organizations as well as individuals. An understanding of these styles can greatly improve creative collaboration.

Furthermore, when a lack of commitment to total quality *programs* surfaces in a work group, it's often interpreted as unjustifiable resistance to a great—and needed—strategic concept. Many times, this resistance is *not* to the *concept* of total quality, but to the *strategy of improvement* embodied in the techniques taught in the program.

Gretchen Price was the director of finance for the Health and Beauty Aids Division of Procter & Gamble. She wanted to apply total quality principles to improve their profit-forecasting system, but she knew her staff had widely divergent views about how to do this. In her words:

> *A senior manager working for me and a young financial manager under him have very different approaches. One likes to modify the "tried-and-true" and the other likes to explore the untried, even radical methods. Typically, on most every financial analysis of a business oppportunity, when they got into conflict, it would become personal, like, "I'm disagreeing with you because you're wrong—and not very smart." It would escalate into something very emotional.*

On the first morning of a two-day conference aimed at redesinging the forecasting process, she introduced a personal assessment questionnaire called the Innovation Styles® Profile and said:

> *I know we'll have a variety of approaches for redoing this forecasting system. Let's take some time to understand those differences and how we can take advantage of the diversity, rather than get bogged down in it.*

---

[1] William Miller, *Fostering Creativity: A Values and Lifestyle Perspective* (Menlo Park, CA: SRI International, 1987).

The Innovation Styles model, to be introduced in this chapter, helped Gretchen's group achieve new levels of synergy not only during the conference, but long afterwards.

> *What we've been able to do is really streamline the process. We even took what, for this particular area in our company culture, were some radical steps like, on judgment, eliminating the frequency of forecasts. The end result is we have a better forecast and people feel a lot better about it.*
>
> *After this seminar, the senior manager and his subordinate sat down and talked from a very personal standpoint. Now at the front end of projects, they are building in the diversity of the styles: "Let's find a way to get some real synergy out of this."*

The results are not unique to Gretchen Price and her staff. This chapter offers a way to bring more synergy and more creativity to bear on the challenges you face, alone or as part of a team.

Two of the classic slogans of total quality are "Do the right thing" and "Do things right." Based on the evolution from TQ to QQ, some people have rephrased these to be "Do things differently" and "Do things better." "Differently" usually means leaping change, whereas "better" means incremental change. Both leaping and incremental innovations are necessary for optimum improvements from quality programs.

Time and again, books and training manuals in total quality reminds us that the most successful practitioners are those who learn how to effectively use analytical and statistical techniques to understand the causes of quality problems and to target process improvements. These analytical tools include

- Cause-and-effect diagram
- Pareto diagram
- Scatter diagram
- Flow diagram
- Histogram

Taken as a group, statistical methods and the analytical skills that make them work are necessary but not complete for continuous learning and improvement. The actual use of these analytical, statistical techniques as lead-ins to idea generation usually emphasize *incremental* improvements.

Leaping changes tend to emphasize starting with intuitive insights, followed by factual verification. Incremental improvements tend to emphasize starting with factual information, which provides fertile ground to subsequently produce intuitive insights. The overarching skill needed is to fluently use intuition to either precede or follow analytical fact finding.

The Modifying and Experimenting styles use the approach of moving from facts to intuition. Thus, as shown in Figure 8.3, incremental solutions emphasize the use of Modifying, with some Experimenting and Visioning. This is well suited to "doing things better." The Visioning and Exploring styles use movement from intuition to facts. Exploring techniques, with some Visioning and Experimenting, are better suited to leaping changes and "doing things differently."

When I was senior consultant for the Innovation Program at SRI International, I facilitated hundreds of innovation sessions to develop innovative new business strategies, technologies, or technology inventions. Some of the idea-generation exercises I gave to a group would be enthusiastically received and productively utilized; others would go nowhere. And most of the time, reaction was mixed: Some found them stimulating and others in the same group didn't. It led me to seriously inquire, "Of the hundred or more idea-generation techniques available through books and one's own imagination, how can we know which ones will work with different people and in different situations?" The Innovation Styles model provided the answer.

Innovation Styles allows you to strategically select and present idea-generation techniques to get everyone involved (using their favored

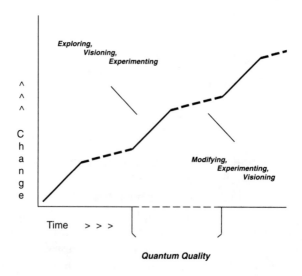

FIGURE 8.3.   Innovation and Change

approaches) and to cover the different approaches—thereby generating a more comprehensive as well as creative set of solutions. By employing all four strategies, there is a much greater opportunity to empower each person to make his or her full contribution—using a variety of styles—and commit to a Quantum Quality solution.

For example, a group of scientists I worked with at Eli Lilly & Company selected the challenge: "How to foster more creativity in our laboratories?" Given the profile of the group, I first led them through a Visioning strategy, followed by a Modifying one.

For the Visioning strategy, I chose the *Future Annual Report* to have them get a snapshot of the future by verbalizing what they really wanted to happen. I told them: "Select a specific project you want to work on. Imagine your company's annual report five years from now, in which there's a page describing your project. As you look over the page—in your imagination—you realize *everything* you wished would happen on this project has come true. What's written there?"

Then, I had them try a Modifying strategy, *Force-Field Analysis*. I told them: "Select one item from your wish list. Complete a force-field analysis by:

1. Expressing your wish as a goal.
2. Describing your best and worst cases.
3. Describing the positive and negative forces that are tugging for and against you.
4. Generating ideas for making the positive forces even stronger or the negative forces weaker."

This technique gave people a sense of practical steps to take with their "blue-sky" wishes.

Then we did an Experimenting technique followed by an Exploring one. (The Exploring technique was last because the group was, for the most part, skeptical of this strategy for new ideas, and I was still building credibility with them.)

For the Experimenting technique, *Matrix Analysis*: "List the two main variables in your issue, and elaborate on the subvariables within those two. Generate ideas for implementing the different cross-relationships between the subvariables attributes."

Guided Imagery was the Exploring method. The purpose of this tool was to find the key for implementing their favorite ideas, making that a key criteria for developing an action plan. I led them through a deep-relaxation exercise and an imaginary dive to the ocean floor to find a special object. Later in the imagery, they walked on the beach and met a wise person, who helped them understand the significance of the symbol they had found.

In this last exercise, many of the workshop participants had very moving and insightful experiences. However, one woman came up to me at the break and complained that the symbol approach to intuition was limiting to her. She explained that she didn't use an intermediary, such as a symbol, to get intuitive insights; "she just got it" in a flash. I realized that she employed her intuition in a Visioning way, to converge on an answer, and the Exploring technique had used intuition to diverge into broader considerations—thus, her difficulty with the method.

In summary, research has identified four distinct strategies for instigating change and finding creative solutions to work challenges: Visioning, Modifying, Experimenting, and Exploring. Eighty percent or more of the techniques for TQM fall into the two strategies of Modifying and Experimenting—leading to a lack of team participation (sometimes by whole functions, such as R&D) and a lack of creative ideas for both incremental and breakthrough solutions.

By working with these different Innovation Styles, you can discover for yourself how you can foster an environment that promotes a greater sense of teamwork and a more comprehensive, creative set of solutions.

Strengthening the System

For the Creative Solution stage the QQ process, there are four more factors for "institutionalizing" a culture for QQ. In this chapter, continuous improvement is based on using four distinct strategies to find creative solutions. Managers and team leaders can empower teams for QQ by aligning the teams on the factors of Idea Support and Idea-Generation Strategies. In the next chapter, continuous improvement is based on making decision based on group values. Managers and team leaders can empower teams for QQ by aligning the teams on the factors of Criteria and the Decision-Making Process.

One key to empowering teams at this stage is developing strong alignment between teams and sponsors to build respect for the free flow of ideas. The other is to employ a range of Innovation Styles strategies and techniques.

I. *Idea Support.* This is the degree to which the team has a sense of community—a cohesion—within the team and with the sponsors. When this is done well, the team deliberately discusses how well it fosters trust and openness with their sponsors, forming a sense of community with their sponsors; agreements between sponsors and the team are kept or renegotiated, and conflicts between the team and sponsors are readily resolved.

J. *Idea-Generation Strategies.* This is the degree to which the team actively uses different idea-generation strategies to help it broaden and deepen the pool of options. When this is done well, the sponsors support the team in using many different strategies to finding creative options and solutions; the team has sufficient time and latitude to allow ideas to develop before judging them.

As sponsors and teams align on these issues, they will foster a culture in which they creatively search for both incremental and breakthrough ideas. Innovations styles, mind-mapping, and affinity diagrams are some of the tools that can help institutionalize this aspect of a positive sponsor-team relationship.

Practicing the Paradigm

Learning

The key question that stimulates and organizes learning in the Creative Solution stage is, "What's value-adding?" When we continually ask, answer, and reask that question, we will learn what we need for creative, continuous improvement based on:

(I) forming effective support for team ideas
(J) using both intuition and analysis for idea generation

The innovative learning organization deliberately develops new ways to broaden the deepen the actual *process* for seeking out and generating new ideas. That process can be a fragile one, given the human tendency to not speak up if there's a chance for embarrassment (or worse): how to give positive encouragement for idea giving; how to purge the NIH virus

("Not Invented Here") from an organization's immune system; how to acknowledge the value of intuition and distinguish it from fantasy wishes; how to use analysis without worshiping it as a false idol. All these are important learning tasks for Quantum Quality.

We can personally inquire, "What do I do that encourages or discourages both myself and others from coming forth with new ideas?" Or, "Under what circumstances do I and others I know feel inspired with our best ideas—and how can I help set up those conditions more often?" As we do, we will find intrinsic ways for participating in a learning community in which we feel, "We search for options using our hearts as well as our minds!"

Values

In the late 1970s, I taught courses on stress and burnout—the long-term erosion of physical, mental, spiritual, and emotional energy. The greatest cause of burnout reported to me was the great outpouring of energy and commitment into a goal and getting absolutely no sense of accomplishment from the effort. Under too much stress, we tend to block out any stimulation or initiative to do something new; we're having enough difficulty just coping with the old. Yet this blocking out can be counterproductive, because it inhibits the creative solutions that can actually alleviate the stress. For creativity to happen, a measure of mental calmness, even in the midst of strenuous external conditions, must be maintained.

While working with brainstorming groups around the world, I've noticed that breakthrough ideas so very often come out of playful and humorous moments. Or they come from "sideline" activities such as jogging, shaving, daydreaming, or whatever, as long as we've had the intention of finding a solution sometime. This requires a letting go of stressful states that cloud the mind and heart from being open to new possibilities—which in turn requires confidence in oneself, one's peers, even one's self-esteem.

In groups, this becomes a shared sense of peace when trust is developed, for example, trust that each person can express his or her ideas, even half-baked ones, without fear of ridicule. Building support for the activity of generating ideas, without regard for the practicality of the ideas, is part and parcel to building this trust and confidence. Then, people will be more likely to state their own personal passion for certain challenge and be motivated to pursue a more breakthrough solution.

Creativity

What creative moments most have in common is a sense of relaxed concentration, where our minds are at peace and we're receptive to an extraordinary or most unusual idea. This sense of inner peace may be in contrast to the hectic pace and stress of today's work life. Cross-culturally, we describe the most creative insights in receptive language rather than active language: phrases like, "It just came to me," "I saw the solution right before my eyes," "I could feel it in my bones," and "The light bulb went off and I knew the answer." This level of receptivity requires a great deal of confidence (*con fides*, literally, "with faith") and trust in the creative process.

As Dr. Joel Levey and Michelle Levey point out so well[2], we need to develop both active and quiet mind skills. Active mind skills include our ability to analyze, visualize, and verbalize. Quiet mind skills include our ability to use imagery and to meditate. Both of these types of skills require a level of inner stillness and peacefulness.

Sustainability

Einstein once said that we cannot find solutions to problems within the same framework that created the problems in the first place. We must find alternatives that break out of the paradigm. Sustainability focuses on ideas for *creating the future we want* rather than repairing past mistakes or merely treating the symptoms of outdated thinking.

To create this better life, we can't wait for the system to change. When faced with the paradoxes and dilemmas of modern society—for example, "How do we redistribute wealth while fostering strong economic growth?"—we can give our attention to what's wrong, and try to problem solve the issues, or we can focus on building the capacities we wish to have for ourselves and our children's children. The former may feel like we're dealing with the issues and expressing a lot of feelings. Yet, the latter has more potential for breaking the habits of thought that keep us reacting to fast-moving events. The more proactive we become, the greater chance we have for building a consensus that's willing to stay even with or ahead of the times.

---

[2] Joel Levey and Michelle Levey, *Quality of Mind* (Boston: Wisdom Pub., 1991).

As Bill Diana of Exxon Chemical reminds us:

To get to the intuitive leap, to reduce the time it takes from conception to commercial reality, honesty and trust have to be at the foundation. There also has to be integrity.

Empowerment is also a growth process. It doesn't happen overnight. You don't walk out in the shop and say you are empowered; it doesn't work that way. In the end, you set up situations where, even if you know the approach that should be taken, you let the team do that.

This is a matter of the heart leading the head, not the other way around. Our quality of life always has been, and will be, based on our understanding and ability to translate the deepest longings and nature of the human spirit into reality. The system will change as a result of creating this better life.

9

Reach Speedy Decisions Based on Group Values

We have put together several "tiger teams"—focused, self-directed teams to crash a particular product through. We shipped two of the products last Friday—little credit-card sized communication adapters that plug into a laptop PC. We cut the cycle of time dramatically, so clearly we made a quantum leap.

—Dennis Kekas, director of Local & Wide Area Network Products, IBM.

Mastering the Mind-Set

In the third stage of the Creative Journey, we generate Creative Solutions in two steps: generating the options and choosing the most valued solution. As shown in Figure 9.1, in this chapter we'll address the principle for choosing the solution in a Quantum Quality way: Reaching speedy decisions based on group values.

We all live and work in fast-moving times. There seems to be no time to stop and think about changing things for the better. We long for a rest, yet we feel we must run faster and faster just to keep up with everyone else. A team must learn to move through the entire Creative Journey quickly but without skipping any steps.

Let's be very clear: speed does not mean being reactive, hasty, or shooting from the hip. If a team rushes prematurely into action, it's just being reactive. Many American companies have hastily put a solution into the market that didn't measure up. It could have used more thought, more quality.

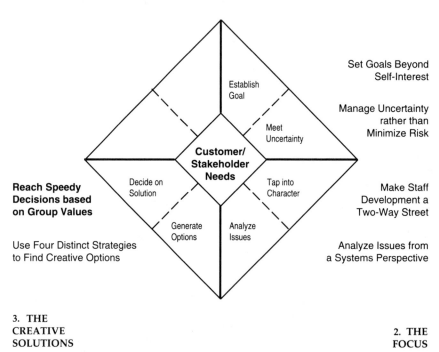

**4. THE
COMPLETION**

**1. THE
CHALLENGE**

Establish
Goal

Meet
Uncertainty

**Customer/
Stakeholder
Needs**

Decide on
Solution

Tap into
Character

Generate
Options

Analyze
Issues

Set Goals Beyond
Self-Interest

Manage Uncertainty
rather than
Minimize Risk

**Reach Speedy
Decisions based
on Group Values**

Make Staff
Development a
Two-Way Street

Use Four Distinct Strategies
to Find Creative Options

Analyze Issues from
a Systems Perspective

**3. THE
CREATIVE
SOLUTIONS**

**2. THE
FOCUS**

FIGURE 9.1. The Creative Journey™

On the other hand, if it bogs down into endless discussions of, "What are we doing here?," or, "Ain't it awful that things are this way?," it's also just being reactive. Both usually end up costing more time and, as captured by the saying, "There's never enough time to do it right, but there's always time to do it over." Some companies overwork their innovation, looking for perfection, always tinkering with it to get it closer to perfect by one more degree. An overemphasis on "hitting home runs" with new ideas and on wanting to have the perfect failure-proof solution both lead to lengthening the development and implementation time. Getting an idea quickly into implementation and then working to make "midcourse corrections" can spur a closer relationship with customers and more frequent, "on-target" updates.

Dennis Kekas runs a billion dollar business developing local and wide area networking products for IBM. He and Rick Morris, his program manager for the PCMCIA[1] adapter, foresaw the fierce competition for this product area. They compiled a team from around the world (some of whom did not report directly to Dennis) and set very aggressive goals to be the first to market with their credit-card sized local area communications adapter. Their original projections were to get to market in 18–20 months. Their new goal was to be shipping full production in 9 months. Getting a prototype to the trade shows in only six months meant Rick, Dennis, and the team needed to take risks. As Rick says,

> We are under a lot of constraints for expense and cost, and there are people very high up in the company looking at things like scrap and rework costs in manufacturing. It used to be that there had to be a whole series of reviews with a number of levels of management before manufacturing could be started. My peers in manufacturing started the manufacturing pipeline, and in order to keep it moving we had to be risking upwards of $100,000 to $150,000 worth of scrap. If that much scrap was produced, Dennis would have had to answer for the loss. We managed the risk carefully because we didn't want to let our leader down.

To be able to make speedy decisions, they needed to lay the groundwork with the rest of the organization. Dennis comments:

> To make a major change in a large organization or company, people have to accept that there is a new way we are going to run the business. Because people understood that this is a changing world and we were trying to do things differently, it made it a little easier sell. Our senior executives said several years ago, "We are going to empower our people. We are going to unshackle them. We are going to turn them loose."
>
> For example, we needed to get the capital equipment approved in a matter of hours instead of weeks, to keep the ball rolling. We had communicated our objective broadly enough and all it took was just a brief explanation of what we're trying to do, why it was important, and they said, "Well, we'll sign up with you." Which was a pleasant surprise.

The team's incentive for working so intensely went well beyond monetary gain. In 1992, they had two of these tiger team efforts completed. In one case, there were up-front incentives for the people and in the other instance they did not. They found the same degree of commitment from

---

[1] Personal Computer Memory Card International Association, which sets the standards for the physical and electrical interfaces that these products adhere to.

both teams. (They rewarded the team that didn't get the up-front incentives). But as Rick tells us,

We had discussions within the team about up-front incentives. Our team specifically said we didn't want people thinking we were doing this for the money—it was a much bigger cause: the competitiveness of IBM and all of the things that our generation has read in the press about big companies not being able to compete. We knew we had some stiff competition and there was a personal challenge at all levels to be able to be the first. IBM has always had its spirit of excellence and wanting to be the best.

Dennis adds,

Some of the team members working on this project did not report directly to me. We had many key engineering and manufacturing activities performed at [two different] facilities abroad. The cooperation and motivation of this team is even more significant when you consider the geographical separation. Corporate management's visible support for our philosophy helped provide a common thread at all three locations.

In spite of all of the enormous pressures that our company has felt, we have tried to preserve our fundamental beliefs, like respect for the individual, excellence in everything that we do. We made a decision to force some action to be taken. In the event that decision may have been wrong, everybody else would rally around to go fix that thing, whereas if you just let it drag on, then you have introduced a delay.

For Rick, that meant running team meetings in a new way.

We were really going to make decisions in those meetings. It quickly changes the quality of the discussion that you have among the team members and their preparedness and their participation in the meetings when they realize that on the spot you are going to make a decision and things are going to move after that. As a group, we said, for example, "What's our confidence factor that this chip will work if we go to silicon now?" We agreed it would be best to go ahead and release the chip and, in parallel, continue to simulate. If our decision was right we have just gained three weeks in the schedule, if it was wrong, well we may have risked some amount of dollars. The team became very good at making decisions that way.

As Dennis describes, the project was a huge success.

We went from start to shipment in about nine months. We showed the product publicly in six months at one of the shows. The rest of it was grinding

through the processes of ordering parts and releasing it. (Previously, something like this would have taken probably eighteen months.) And we came in millions of dollars under budget.

It was kind of amazing how positive the press was. "Maybe they are for real, serious about being first."

Rick and his team aren't just sitting back on the glory, however.

Our team, of course, is celebrating all the accolades we're getting, but at the same time we're being self-critical enough to say, "What did we do wrong this time." And we did make some mistakes. It is not coming from management that says, "Well, you were great guys, but you also made some mistakes." It is coming from within the team that says, "How can we do this better?" But that is part of the cultural change.

One of the learnings that has emerged from debriefing the success of IBM's tiger teams is that each individual can say, "I contributed that part." And for speed and values to play this significant role in business success, fear needs to disappear. Rick comments:

We had one guy writing the software and we told him, "Brian, whatever you make this software is what it's going to be. If you make it good it's going to be good, if you do lousy it's going to be lousy, but whatever you make it is what it's going to be." He knew he didn't have ten people looking over his shoulder.

Dennis adds:

There was nobody to hide behind either. If he really made a mistake he was pretty visible. Even if the management wasn't aware of the truth, the rest of the team members knew where the mistake was made. And if it was done unintentionally, it was one of those things that happen. But if you slacked off and you failed that would be pretty visible too and you'd take a lot of personal heat for that.

Even though there was much greater exposure in terms of people's accountability and therefore of risk, there wasn't an atmosphere of fear. Rather, there was a sense of real collaboration and responsibility. As Dennis says:

We never threatened, never put the fear factor. We just said let's do the best we can. That is all we can ask you to do with these aggressive schedules. If we blow them a little bit, we're in it with you.

As Rick describes, the role of management in promoting this productive level of risk-taking is quite profound.

> *When you first realize that now you are empowered there is this initial fear of the responsibility that goes along with empowerment. The role senior management needs to play is to nurture you through that period of fear. Once the people get over that initial shock of, "Holy mackerel, I really am empowered," then they start to grow tremendously and they practice skills they didn't even realize they had and tackle jobs that even they didn't feel they could tackle.*

This empowerment is one-third of what makes this tiger team so successful, as Dennis summarizes.

> *A key element of the success of this program was that the team developed a focus that was completely market-driven. They had a close eye on the competition, and had direct contact with customers to validate requirements. With a quick development cycle-time they could satisfy the requirements before they changed. The three elements—market driven requirements, cycle-time reduction, and empowerment—are closely linked.*

In the past few years, "cycle time reduction"—cutting down the throughput time by making a process different or better—has become almost synonymous with continuous improvement. As markets change faster and faster, a more demanding issue than reducing "cycle time" is reducing "break-even time." At issue is the reduction of time from initial product concept to a profit break-even point. Cycle time is an internal improvement process. The latter involves customer behavior (paying for the product).

As noted in Chapter One, John Young, Hewlett-Packard's CEO, issued a series of three directives to the whole company during his tenure: 10× product quality, 10× software quality, and achievement of a 50 percent reduction in break-even time. Notice that this went beyond reducing cycle time.

One difference between cycle time and break-even time is the difference between efficiency and effectiveness. Patricia Moore, former manager of Organization Consulting Services at Hewlett-Packard, elaborates on this:

> *The underlying question is, "Why are we here?" And if you are talking about effectiveness—not efficiency, but effectiveness—that question is answered by our customers.*
>
> *Efficiency is the internal focus of how much better can we do what we're doing? Effectiveness is the external focus: What is it our customers want*

from us, and what is their definition of value? What are their obstacles? What are the things that will help them overcome them? And, then, how can we back up the chain to help our people satisfy their need to satisfy their customer needs?

Effective speed comes from being proactive: looking for opportunities to anticipate unspoken notions of providing customer value—delighting the customers and stakeholders. To gain effectiveness in making decisions that provide value to customers, the efficiency must go into the decision-review and decision-making process. And speed in the decision process goes all the way back to the design process. Whereas some might think that this speedup could hurt quality, research has shown it can actually *improve* product and operational quality.

One of the seeming dilemmas of the corporate 1990s is the need for downsizing and re-engineering. Hailed as essential for global competitiveness, it also has its limitations. As George Stalk and Tom Hout, vice presidents with the Boston Consulting Group, have written:

Restructuring and time compression are different kinds of transformations. Restructuring is essentially a reductive process, a sorting down of businesses and procedures, a compression of activities around fewer people. The road to faster cycle times is a more integrative process. Time compression gets started by making more connections and seeing more of the whole.

Quality standards are not enough. Cost controls are not enough. Neither are work teams, long work hours, downsizing, or re-engineering. To achieve sustainable advantage, people within your company must continually serve customers in new ways, re-invent their jobs, and develop new products and services.[2]

Genichi Taguchi has pointed out quite clearly that quality begins with the effectiveness of the design process, which then makes quality improvement more efficient further down the development/production/marketing/service line. We can then actualize a sense of purpose and vision for making a significant contribution to our stakeholders and to ourselves.

Taguchi's definition of quality—minimizing the cost to society when products don't meet stakeholder needs—can be expanded to include what we contribute to society, rather than just to ourselves, inspiring us to

---

[2] George Stalk Jr. and Thomas Hout, *Competing Against Time* (New York: Macmillan, 1990), p. 264–265, 271.

reach for decisions that improve the quality of everyone's lives. For years, we have talked about the "Quality of Life" and how it might be defined: "The amount of material goods"? "A healthy family"? "Spiritual richness"? "GNP and economic growth"? Quality of Life includes having managers who listen and nurture their staff's creative best, rather than motivating through fear, punishing mistakes, or making decisions by command-and-control methods.

This leads us to other aspect of the process (besides speed) for making effective decisions for Quantum Quality: the *commitment* to implementing a decision. Making decisions based purely on the numbers may seem to be the easy, most expeditious way of meeting the speed factor. The mirage in that way of thinking is the commitment factor, which brings up the question of investing our personal values in our work.

At Hewlett-Packard, research on the 200 "most exceptional" managers revealed many common traits including the use of specific statements of team/group values in decision making. They found that when a team and its management made a decision that embodied their own personal values (not only the published corporate values), there was more than mere compliance to a decision. There was actual commitment to making that decision work.

When we believe in a decision with our hearts, not just our minds, we put all our efforts into making it happen. We persist beyond the norm to listen to the impact our decision might have on other stakeholders. We find a solution we cannot only "live with," but can also embrace as "This is what we stand for."

Using core values as decision criteria—more than just "What do the numbers say?"—can inspire commitment rather than simply compliance. This commitment comes from intrinsic rather than extrinsic satisfactions.

For Herman Maynard, business consultant and former manager of business development for DuPont's Wire and Cable Division, *trust* is the key value for making decisions that engender commitment from the people who implement them.

> *When you start building trust, people are willing to do the right thing, not just comply with what they are told to do. For sure, there may be more opportunities for embarrassment. . . . But there will be a lot more opportunities to create value.*

Sometimes making the right decision means redefining the context and building trust instead of fear.

Prior to my assignment in the Wire & Cable Division, we had a situation where a business was losing about $10 million a year and we were getting ready to sell it off. We found in talking with people that we had all this equipment sitting in the warehouse but not installed because someone up the line had this dictated that you couldn't add capacity. Now, the plant had been sold out for years and of course the equipment was already there in the warehouse and had been there for 3–4 years.

We redefined the project to install the equipment as a cost-savings project instead of a capacity project. The payback was less than two weeks and the next year's earnings were $10 million positive, a $20 million after-tax turnaround. We did what everybody knew was the right thing to do. Quite simply, the reason people had not done this before was fear of angering the boss at each step up the line.

In another situation, the *turnaround* of their cable business depended on this trust and love.

We were able to reduce time to commercialization from over three years to less than three months; this is from the time of the initial idea to introducing it in the marketplace. We were able to increase productivity of our technical and marketing staff over 500 percent. In addition, we went from a position where we were losing market share and earnings in every major product line to where we were growing at five times the industry average. Our earnings over a three-year period increased threefold.

What made the difference was that we created an atmosphere of trust. We put almost all of our management energy into addressing the needs of our people, and creating a vision and a set of values that we all believed in. We placed our attention on people and their growth, on customers and servicing their needs. And as a business unit, we said we are going to take risks: "We're going to decide on what's right for the customer, and if we do that correctly, we're going to be rewarded."

Trust is built in many ways. I remember the enormous impact when a key manager stood up in front of a sales meeting of about thirty people and said, "I love each and everyone of you and I will do everything in my power to support you." There was silence. All of a sudden, we had a different world.

I think at the ultimate level, it really does come out of that kind of commitment to love and support.

Our values are reflected in the process of reaching a decision as well as the content of the decision. The process we use shows as much about our values as the content does, and is more the measure for others to judge whether we're willing to act according to our beliefs and values. When we show consistency, people will trust our participation in decisions, will respect our integrity, and be more willing to engage in true collaborative decision making.

This leads to different management behavior. The whole thing has driven middle management crazy because it has totally redefined their jobs from being information filters and synthesizers to being a coach. Herman adds:

> *I think the enlightened manager is going to see his role as serving people. His job will be to help people understand uncertainty and options, and then be able to give the support they need to make the best decision.*
>
> *If managers focus on coaching, questioning, probing, strengthening people, then just by asking questions and saying where they can get support, they're giving up control.*

Therefore, making decisions based on speed and values requires a real shift in consciousness about *how* we engage with others to blend different values and interests. Robert Selman at Harvard University has described at least three different levels of decision making, which parallel psychological maturity. The least mature is *impulsive,* where we have a desire and seek to meet it as quickly as possible; there is little consideration for others in this approach. The second is *trade-offs,* where we seek trade offs, sacrificing what we want at one time to get what we want another time; there is consideration for others only to the extent that it serves our own needs. The third is *collaboration,* where we seek a mutually win–win solution; there is equal consideration of others, for a solution must fulfill both as much as possible.

We can actually practice and develop our deepest values to develop a richer quality of life for all of us and still be successful in the "real world." This "real world" success can actually *depend* on value-based decisions for long-term growth, whether we are American software developers, Japanese bankers, European car manufacturers, African miners, or Argentinian ranchers. It's a new way to think of the maxim, "Be in the world, but not of it."

Strengthening the System

In addition to the factors described in the previous chapter—Idea Support and Idea Generation Strategies—managers and team leaders can empower teams in the Creative Solutions stage by aligning the teams on the factors of Criteria and Decision-Making Process.

One key to empowering quality teams at this stage is establishing decision-making criteria that are based on group values and that include "speed" as a make-or-break issue. The other is shortening the time for ideas to be developed, reviewed, and decided upon.

K. *Criteria.* This is the degree to which the team and the sponsors have agreement on the most important qualitative and quantitative criteria for assessing the creative options. When this is done well, the team understands the sponsor's qualitative and quantitative criteria for evaluating alternatives, with a clear relationship to the key success factors and to team/sponsor's values; the team and sponsors both actively employ intuition and data analysis in applying their criteria, using more qualitative criteria early in the process and more quantitative criteria later.

L. *Decision-Making Process.* This is the degree to which the team and the sponsors have a satisfactory process for assessing which alternatives meet the criteria in the short-term and the long-term. When this is done well, the team understands the players, the steps, and the milestones in the decision-making process, with structured methods for evaluating alternatives; the team and sponsors get the participation of a variety of people and viewpoints for evaluating, with a means for "storing," rejected ideas that might have new potential in the future.

As sponsors and teams align on these two issues, they will foster a culture in which they develop win–win solutions that inspire commitment rather than compliance. Opportunity mapping, electronic consensus building, and values-based decision matrices are some of the tools that can help institutionalize this aspect of a positive sponsor-team relationship.

Practicing the Paradigm

Learning

As we've seen, the key question that stimulates and organizes learning in the Creative Solution stage is, "What's value-adding?," which includes not only "What options do we seek?," but also "What's the most valued choice to make?"

Chapter Eight stated that in asking, "What options do we seek?," we must learn how to:

(I) form effective support for team ideas
(J) use both intuition and analysis for idea generation

For "What are the key issues and priorities?," we must learn how to:

(K) apply varying qualitative/quantitative criteria at different times
(L) employ well-understood steps for moving new concepts through the system

People in a true learning organization have a clear understanding of the criteria to be applied in any decision-making process. These criteria must take into account the values and interests of the decision makers, the implementers, the organization, and the broader stakeholders. Learning about the relationship between decisions made, the criteria they were chosen by, and the impact on stakeholders is a key learning task. Learning about the most expeditious process for reviewing ideas and coming to decisions—not killing ideas that are worthy and not keeping ideas alive that are not aligned with key success factors—is another. Sharing those learnings with everyone in the organization helps to create the *innovative* learning community.

To strengthen the personal impact we can have on this process, we can ask ourselves, "What personal values are important for me to have represented by any decision (before I'll be fully committed to it)?" or "How open or resistant am I to evaluating my pet ideas (whether by myself or others) based on analysis and intuition?" By developing our own capacity to be open, intuitive, and analytical, we can learn the deeper art of successful decision making. Then we can feel, "We're committed to what we choose!"

Values

Inner peace also finds expression in one's ability to allow diversity and freedom, even in the midst of serious decision making. This freedom actually comes from a deep commitment to finding breakthrough solutions: looking at even the most unconventional solutions before picking the optimum one, not stopping until an issue is fully solved, and staying focused on the goals while relaxing in the process.

This freedom to search is not limited by time or resources. It is not held back by asking,"How can we continue doing what's worked in the past?" Using the motivation of setting goals beyond self-interest, it freely involves perspectives even from competing interests. Using the insights from systemic analysis, it looks beyond treating symptoms to finding solutions for long-term optimum health.

Ultimately, this freedom also comes from choosing only those solutions where one can say, "I'm at peace with this decision. This will serve our stakeholders. This is something that is aligned with my values."

Creativity

The creative process is a breathing rhythm between divergence and convergence, opening to new possibilities and selecting the most valuable ones. The decision-making process, therefore, feeds the creative mind when the timing is right: not killing ideas inappropriately and not letting ideas string along when they should be set aside.

Perhaps, the greatest application of creativity to the actual decision-making process is finding ways to get all the key contributors to say their full truth; not compromise their true values; and look beyond themselves for a solution that everyone can commit to rather than comply with. This demands a great skill and maturity in creative relationships.

Sustainability

Sustainability requires that we *make quality choices based more on qualitative measures* than on quantitative ones. We often try to control company growth by planning, executing, and measuring results purely on quantitative terms. When we do this, we are led down a certain path of decision making that emulates the "centrally planned economy" type of thinking—and we've seen what that produces. In fact, in October 1990, 3,000 managers from eastern and western Europe met in Prague to discuss "Strategic Management and Innovation." Dr. Henry Mintzberg, a professor of management at McGill University in Montreal described how the events in eastern Europe in 1989 demonstrated to everyone that centrally planned economies don't work: They don't foster initiative, innovation, or productivity.

However, he added, when we look at many prime examples of "free enterprise giants" among western corporations, they've often operated as centrally planned economies within a single company (instead of country)—and that they don't foster initiative, innovation, or productivity either, thus becoming less competitive in the global market.

His caution to the eastern Europeans was sobering: As they import western management practices, "Watch out for what you import." Many practices may seem familiar, and that's trouble for both sides. This is especially true with an overemphasis on accounting and control—which actually undermines accountability and empowerment.

Finding creative, high-quality solutions to developing and delivering the IBM PCMCIA adapter card required breaking old habits of how things were decided. According to Dennis Kekas:

Habits restrict awareness, and old habits are the things that cause you not to see breakthroughs. It is just part of our human nature. And I think here what we did is we broke a lot of habits about a way to do things that had been good for a different era. So there is now a new standard of excellence.

10

Assume Leadership and Managership at All Levels

At Fairchild, I was running the development side of our MIS organization, with all the application developers and systems software people (the highest paid people in the organization). I had grown up with programmers, so I was kind of an elitist. My most frequent complaint was about the people in the computer room. (I had never known them, so let's be clear about how much I knew.) One day, the computer operations manager left and I was the one who was asked to take his place. I was devastated.

> —Carlene Ellis, corporate vice president, Intel Corporation

Mastering the Mind-Set

In the fourth stage of the Creative Journey, we head toward Completion in two steps: implementing the creative solution and celebrating the results of what was achieved and learned. As shown in Figure 10.1, in this chapter, we'll address the principle for implementing solutions in a Quantum Quality way: Making implementation a "community" affair.

It only took me a month to figure out that the idiots screwing up the computer room were the programmers that worked in my old organization. They were writing code that hung up all the jobs. It was the blind leading the blind. One of the first things I implemented was that the programmers had to come in and run their jobs "on the store" before we'd accept them in production.

I believe that you put an animal or person or anything else in a box, and you're going to get box behavior and you're going to get a punch, counter-punch mentality to your business. All along, I've had a mind-set that a

133

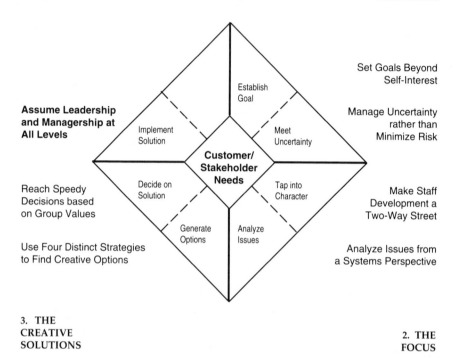

4. THE
COMPLETION

1. THE
CHALLENGE

Set Goals Beyond
Self-Interest

Establish
Goal

**Assume Leadership
and Managership at
All Levels**

Manage Uncertainty
rather than
Minimize Risk

Implement
Solution

Meet
Uncertainty

**Customer/
Stakeholder
Needs**

Reach Speedy
Decisions based
on Group Values

Decide on
Solution

Tap into
Character

Make Staff
Development a
Two-Way Street

Generate
Options

Analyze
Issues

Use Four Distinct Strategies
to Find Creative Options

Analyze Issues from
a Systems Perspective

3. THE
CREATIVE
SOLUTIONS

2. THE
FOCUS

FIGURE 10.1.   The Creative Journey™

group of human beings, unboxed (which is key) can really get done anything that can be understood. You really have to believe that people are innately good, they come to work because they want to work, they come to work because they want to do great things. Your deal is to unleash them to do great things.

Carlene realized that the computer room employees were "boxed in." All they wanted was to get things to work right. Once they understood that they had a manager who was going to support their every concern, and once they knew that they were going to get a lot of praise yet be held accountable for making it work, they did things that they never thought they could do. They assumed "managership" of the computer room.

I said, "What else do you guys think we should do?" They responded, "We don't need all these people in the computer room checking what we're doing . . . there's a shift supervisor, then there's his boss, and then there's you and

we're not sure what you do at all." I said, "You probably don't need three lev-
els of management checking on one, do you? You guys run it. If you can't
handle something by yourself, come out and get us."

Obviously, we had some failures; obviously, some stuff didn't work. But,
over time, the guys became a self-sufficient unit. It would be like a manufac-
turing facility being run with no managers on the floor, literally, which was
unheard of in that industry at that time. All I could see was the possibility of
making it better, because I knew that they knew when there's some way to
add value and what boxes them in.

Perhaps most impressively, they gained the confidence to assume leadership in taking over duties that only systems software people were able to
do before.

I went to my old systems software group and said see how much of your job,
like routine maintenance, you can turn over to them, so you can go do the
high-tech stuff. Take the bottom low end of your job and give it to them. You
can do more; they can do more; we can do more.

They did it. The operators got to a point that they would routinely send
out messages to the programmers on how to improve their systems, which
they never would have done.

So I saw these operators who ran the computer room—I can get very
emotional about this—become something I thought they had never been. I
ended up with these nonexempt, hourly employees doing a long-range plan
for the computer room, and they were hourly people making under $20,000 a
year. We have got to open up their eyes, their ears, and their mouth so that
they can tell us.

The title to this chapter is purposely a pun. To assume means to take on,
to take responsibility, as in "to assume command." It also means to presume, to take for granted, as in "to assume he/she is capable of. . . ." Both
are appropriate for the step of implementing a creative quality solution.

We must be willing to take personal responsibility for taking leadership and managership roles, no matter what hierarchical position we find
ourselves in. We must also take for granted that people throughout the
hierarchy have the potential for exercising leadership and managership.
Both of these types of "assuming" can be self-fulfilling prophecies:
Assume leadership and we become leaders; assume managership and we
become managers (in *deed* if not in formal role); assume the potential in
others and we see it actualized in them.

Carlene puts it this way:

In my new job, what I believe I need to do is "turn the heartlight on" in every Intel employee, that they can change the way Intel works permanently for the better. I think if we can do that, some changes will fail, some will win, it'll be fine. Some won't fit together; some will. I think we'll have a very different company in the next decade if we can just pursue that line of thought.

Assuming leadership and managership makes implementation truly a "community affair," which is much more than simply getting everyone involved. It's an entire attitude that mirrors the first stage of the Quantum Quality process: setting goals that are beyond self-interest. It's a pursuit of excellence where it counts most: in really putting the best ideas of every employee *to work.*

Mike Szymanczyk, who has served as a senior executive in several multinational corporations including Procter & Gamble, Kraft General Foods, and Philip Morris USA, was interviewed by consultant Juanita Brown about consciously using the "community development" model to describe a healthy business growth.[1] He said,

Most business models are highly competitive models. Basically people are working their own agenda in an effort to succeed in the competition against the criteria that top management has set up. Some of that is productive to business and a bunch of it isn't. The community model starts from a different place. The community has a purpose rather than a criteria. Rather than the people serving a master, even a benevolent master, they are serving a common purpose. The community model is a systemic approach driven by the whole, and the traditional business model is a more segmented approach, driven by a few. It's a major structural difference.

When values-based differences (in defining the purpose) exist unresolved, the leadership has a tough job. Our primary role as leaders is to understand what our employees and the other constituencies want as their purpose. We facilitate communication, including listening. Our job is to remove obstacles by seeing that structures and decision processes are well-aligned with the company's purpose.

Last year, I was visiting the corporate offices of Levi Strauss, the jeans and clothing people, I was told about a project to recreate the history of the company through the eyes of the "oldtimers." The company had always

---

[1] Juanita Brown, "Corporation as Community," in *New Traditions in Business* (San Francisco: Sterling and Stone, 1991), p. 142–144.

been very successful, and they wanted to chronicle that success. They interviewed retired executives and staff from as long ago as they could (the company was started in 1849, so they missed out on some).

What struck the interviewers, and me, was that the former employees rarely spoke of this or that great market share, or big profits, or beating up the competition. Their best memories were the relationships they shared while working together. The relationships made their time with the company seem worthwhile, almost as if the job tasks, in retrospect, weren't important in themselves but as the "excuse" for sharing close relationships.

On this notion of assuming leadership and managership, Toyota and General Motors formed a joint venture (NUMMI) in Fremont CA at a plant that GM had closed due to poor labor relations. Using Japanese-style quality management practices, it now has labor productivity 50% higher than other GM plants; yet 85% of the labor force worked at the plant before the joint venture was formed. It shows what is possible when these principles[2] are actualized:

1. *Kaizen*, the never ending quest for perfection
2. Develop full human potential
3. Pursuit of superior quality
4. Build mutual trust
5. Develop team performance
6. Provide a stable environment
7. *Every employee a manager.* . . Good thinking equals good products. Accept responsibility yourself for all matters relating to your company.

However, this principle of employee-as-manager can run into a great deal of resistance. Bruce Lee, director of the United Auto Worker's western region, has stated, "The lessons of NUMMI's success are still being resisted by executives, plant managers, and foremen who see their authority threatened by the idea of power sharing."[3]

But is all resistance to change due to feeling threatened? Could even the resistance to quality improvement principles spring from something else in the minds and feelings of managers and employees? This is an important question if we are to collaborate rather than compete internally for developing the most effective work processes.

---

[2] As stated in the NUMMI team member handbook
[3] Quoted in Jerry Bowles and Joshua Hammond, *Beyond Quality* (New York: G. P. Putnam's Sons, 1991), p. 187.

When a new idea is proposed, a great deal of resistance is often anticipated, planned for, managed, "overcome," or "succumbed to." As former
director of Hewlett-Packard Laboratories, Frank Carrubba, says:

> *A transition in management usually means that there's going to be changes,*
> *and those changes can be frightening. People can have a particular capability*
> *and credibility, a good understanding of their field, they understand their*
> *customers really well . . . and suddenly they're going to be asked to start over.*
> *They're going to have to sort of leap out and grab onto something new and*
> *know that while they're leaping there's no way of turning around and going*
> *back.*

What is the nature of this resistance to change? A dictionary definition of
change is "to cause to be different; alter; transform; to exchange or replace
by another."[4] All organizations go through many changes—reorganizations, automation, personnel turnover, and so and on. Change often
brings paradoxical feelings of excitement, fear, longing, or even anger,
especially when change is introduced at work. The way the change
process is managed often makes the transition more painful than necessary, prompting the perceptions that "We're falling apart!" or "Management doesn't know how to manage."

One of the biggest frustrations for managers who try to implement the
total quality dimension of "team empowerment" is the resistance many
employees give to the extra personal responsibility of empowerment.
Resistance to this type of change, or any organizational change, can come
from a number of sources:

- *Integrity.* We might resist a proposed change out of a sincere belief that
  it is not the highest good for the people or the problem. This resistance
  is strengthened when the status quo would be hard to reestablish if
  the change effort failed. We press for a solution that our hearts know is
  better.

- *Fear.* We might resist change when we perceive it might threaten our
  jobs, status, dignity, budgets, or relationships. We don't trust that the
  change is really in our best interests. Sometimes this fear may be justi-
  fied. At other times, it may be a "victim" mentality that doesn't like
  others "controlling" our lives. Anger and frustration may spring from
  the base emotion of fear.

---

[4] *American Heritage Dictionary* (Boston: Houghton Mifflin, 1985), p. 224.

- *Communication.* We might resist change due to a lack of understanding of the need for change. This can prevent any serious cooperation, particularly when the price seems too high. A too forceful style of telling people what to do can offend, leading to the same result.

- *History.* We might resist change if we have experienced many meaningless and poorly implemented changes or if we lack confidence in the abilities of the sponsors and change agents to make it work. This resistance is compounded by poor communications.

- *Pace.* We might resist change when we don't have enough time to grieve the passing of the way things used to be. The experience of loss and letting go heals at its own pace. Winters are a necessary time and cannot be hurried before a springtime can occur.

- *Stress.* We might resist change when there already is too much stimulation for us to manage. We'd rather keep the problems we're familiar with than undergo possible turmoil to get to a "promised land."

The number one issue for responding to these resistances is *trust*, dealing with any fears that others may feel. This means—for everyone, not just formal managers—handling situations without fear being the motivational tactic used. It also means sharing power. Carlene Ellis has found this to be essential to her success:

> To teach empowerment, you actually have to teach a manager how not to manage through fear. And if a manager doesn't manage through fear, then you don't need to teach the employees empowerment. I must say that fifty times at Intel, "Why are you asking permission?" "Well, I didn't know what someone would think." "Who cares; don't ask permission. Go do it, and we'll figure out later if it's a big problem."
>
> The more power I can give away to people and the less power I'm perceived to have, then I can run around and break down barriers for people because they think it was all their idea. They're just out there implementing their own stuff.

Herman Maynard, former manager of business development at DuPont's Wire and Cable Division, tells this story:

> We had this new business development group with many successes from a production point of view. We were creating wealth at a very rapid rate. Unfortunately, people were so energetic that their stress levels were going up. We knew something had to be done.

To reduce stress levels, we set three new priorities: first, safety, health, and family; second, spend a minimum of 20 percent of one's time learning; and third, after the first two priorities are satisfied, work towards accomplishment of the business mission. In essence, don't do anything that puts your personal safety or anyone else's safety at risk. Do what you need to be healthy. Pay attention to your family—family comes before work. If your daughter's play or going to a customer dinner are in conflict, and you're struggling with the answer, go to the daughter's play. Each person was responsible for selecting what learning area or areas they would focus on, how they would go about it, and—importantly—without management oversight. Finally, another priority was set to spend a minimum of 20 percent of their time learning.

It took us three months on average before individuals believed we were really serious. And this was with a group of empowered people. What we found was that productivity reached the highest levels ever and we could not discern any difference in the level of expenditure or the amount of time people spent on the job. The number of times that there was a conflict was actually very small. And, yes, stress levels did go down.

There is also a larger rhythm for which we are to be sensitive. Organizational growth follows a breathing pattern of expansion and consolidation that corresponds to exhaling and inhaling. When an organization has successfully stabilized a new business with centralized decision making and functional roles (inhaling), the time eventually comes for more decentralization (exhaling). And when decentralization has succeeded in establishing a broader growth pattern for the company (exhaling), there is often a need for more consolidation (inhaling).

The very structure and culture needed to make one stage succeed can become a barrier to later growth. Not realizing this, we often hold back when the limits of one stage have been reached and the next stage is calling for a change in management practices. A typical response is, "Since our old way of managing has worked so far, we just need to do it better." Such resistance to change can take any number of forms:

- Being unwilling to take risks
- Dwelling on internal competition
- Remaining focused on short-term goals and operations
- Assigning creativity to a single group, like R&D
- Emphasizing control in the face of uncertainty ("Guarantee to me that this will work")

This amounts to the organization "holding its breath." On the other hand, we can also exhale for too long. Change for the sake of change, or change in continual reaction to the environment, eventually diminishes productive energy at all levels. We need a point of stability during change, an anchor of constancy. This is best supplied by an organization's purpose and our commitment to fulfilling that purpose.

Strengthening the System

In the Completion stages, there are four final factors for sustaining Quantum Quality at all levels of the organization. In this chapter, continuous improvement is based on implementing solutions for excellence, not perfection. Managers and team leaders can empower teams for QQ by aligning the teams on factors of Resource Allocation and Transition Management. In the next chapter, continuous improvement is based on rewarding focused learning as well as improvement. Managers and team leaders can empower teams for QQ by aligning the teams on Impact Appraisal and Satisfaction/ Rewards.

One key to empowering quality teams at this stage is providing a well-communicated channel for gaining needed resources (time, money, information). The other is carefully managing the change/transition process when implementing solutions to quality problems.

M. *Resource Allocation.* This is the degree to which the team has the necessary resources—time, money, information—that it needs to implement the solution. When this is done well, the sponsors have made sufficient resources available for the team to apply for, including access to special funds for pilot projects, through a well-understood process; the team is able to apply budget procedures to help justify requested resources.

N. *Transition Management.* This is the degree to which the team has a plan for introducing the organizational changes that are needed to implement the solution successfully. When this is done well, the team is able to construct detailed plans—who, what, when—for a speedy implementation that elicits the buy-in of key people; the team knows how to address resistance to new ideas, in their sponsors and others, working together to implement plans without a significant drop in productivity.

As sponsors and teams align on these two issues, they will foster a culture in which they work diligently to ensure their best solutions are implemented without fail. Organization effectiveness, project planning, and negotiating processes are some of the tools that can help institutionalize this aspect of a positive sponsor-team relationship.

Practicing the Paradigm

Learning

The key question that stimulates and organizes learning in the Creative Solution stage is, "What's working?" This question can lead us to learn what we need for creative, continuous improvement based on:

(N) having access to sufficient financial, human, and time resources

(O) participating in planning and implementing organizational change

This is the time to see if we "put our money where our mouth is"—to provide the implementation resources if a solution really fits with what we say we want. This means paying attention to different views of the resource needs and learning how to negotiate and share the use of scarce resources (to serve the larger whole). In an organization where learning is shared across all functions, then those responsible to fulfilling the implementation plans will know what they need to meet the "local needs and interests" when planning the implementation. This shared learning is essential for implementation to be a "community affair."

To be honest with ourselves and our level of supporting "community" implementation, we can ask, "How freely do I share resources under my control in service to the larger whole (beyond my self interest)?" "How well do I listen for the impact of my plans on others—and seek out the possible wisdom of their resistance?" This line of inquiry can open us to finding the "easy path" through the jungle of implementation, which makes it ironical yet deeply true that then we can feel, "We persevere to the very end!"

Values

The key value to emphasize here is Right Action: making sure our actions are in line with what we stand for and what we're capable of: our *response ability*. This can be difficult because the implementation can be, for some, the most stressful and discouraging time of a project. This is a time to tap back into one's character and courage—literally one's heart—and reach out to make connections with all the people who might be resistant to change, might want to control the change, or might have a better idea for change.

This is also a time to remember what it means to administer an implementation plan. It means to "minister to" the ultimate beneficiaries of our work—the internal/external customers and stakeholders. To minister to another doesn't have to mean self-sacrifice; it means to be emboldened to involve them in actions that rightly embody the spirit of well-being, truth, peace.

When people are resistant, and behave in ways that might endanger the project, it's easy to be sensitive to one's *pet idea* being rejected. A deeper sensitivity would be to feel as one's own feeling the emotions of the others.

Creativity

Perhaps the most demanding part of the Creative Journey is figuring out how to finish getting the buy-in and active assistance for implementing an idea. They so often have so many ramifications for the rest of the work unit or whole organization. This is also where "the rubber meets the road" and the creative idea has to bear fruit or be discarded. This can be a threat to self-esteem and personal performance, and some people shy away from risking the possibility of failure (thus increasing the likelihood).

Sustainability

There is no one person or one group that has a lock on what it takes to create a sustainable, healthy, and wealthy global community. Sustainability requires that we *achieve progress through influence and participation*, not authority, in righting the problems we face. And this process sometimes defies an emotional rush to implement the first "reasonable" solution, usually in a hurried, command-and-control fashion.

Indeed, there is the danger of trying to minimize the task of organizational change with quick-fix solutions and overly simple programs. The transformation of our work groups, organizations, and larger units of society requires a critical mass of support, though not necessarily a majority. The transformation can emerge quite suddenly after the temperature of change has worked up (sometimes subtly) to the boiling point. It might also emerge quite slowly, an evolution that we might wish would progress rapidly yet will not be hurried.

Sustainable change also has its own breathing rhythm. For us to "hold our breath"—to ignore the need for change or the rhythm of change—means eventual unconsciousness and bare survival at best. To anticipate and embrace necessary change is to breathe long and deeply, thriving instead of merely surviving.

Ed McCracken, CEO of Silicon Graphics, agrees that this requires a confident, calm, inner character—that can elicit the same in others. How does he work to develop this in himself?

> *I meditate each day. I find that it is an important part of my life. I think it is important to access your more intuitive side, that part of you that feels real even with the unreality associated with the computer industry. It gives you a more balanced point to operate from, and the result is more risk-taking, less anxiety and less need to try to control everything.*

His model is a good one for anyone and everyone who would "assume leadership and managership at all levels."

11

Reward Focused Learning as Well as Improvement

One of the teams was doing a fantastic job when a technician doing a study made an observation that the livers of these animals had an abnormality. His supervisor did another study, and checked the work we'd done thirteen weeks back. She found that cholesterol was getting trapped in the liver, which meant we had to bring an end to this project.

—Frank Douglas, executive vice president of R&D, Marion Merrill Dow, speaking of a project at Ciba Geigy Pharmaceutical

Mastering the Mind-Set

In the fourth stage of the Creative Journey, we fulfill the Completion stage in two steps: implementing the creative quality solution and gaining satisfaction from tangible (measureable) and intangible results. As shown in Figure 11.1, in this chapter we'll address the principle for the gaining satisfaction in a Quantum Quality way: Rewarding focused learning as well as achievements.

The compound Frank was talking about was one he had pushed for many years, even before he had taken over the Research Department. With the determination that the compound was depositing cholesterol in the liver, which could lead to extensive liver damage, his reputation was at stake, as was the morale of the scientific team that was working on it. In addition, it had had a high potential for being a huge winner in the marketplace.

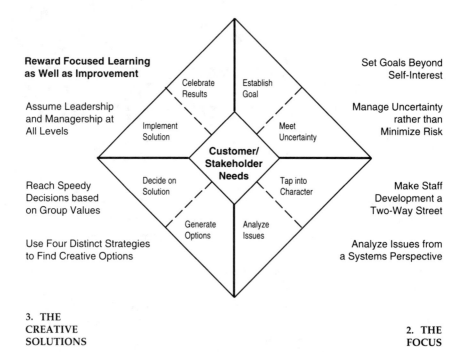

4. THE COMPLETION

1. THE CHALLENGE

Reward Focused Learning as Well as Improvement

Set Goals Beyond Self-Interest

Assume Leadership and Managership at All Levels

Manage Uncertainty rather than Minimize Risk

Reach Speedy Decisions based on Group Values

Make Staff Development a Two-Way Street

Use Four Distinct Strategies to Find Creative Options

Analyze Issues from a Systems Perspective

3. THE CREATIVE SOLUTIONS

2. THE FOCUS

Celebrate Results — Establish Goal — Implement Solution — Meet Uncertainty — Customer/Stakeholder Needs — Decide on Solution — Tap into Character — Generate Options — Analyze Issues

FIGURE 11.1.   The Creative Journey™

It was the most exciting project we had coming out during my period of leadership. This compound was about to go into phase three. If it had made it to the market, it would have been significant because it was a different mechanism and potentially a significant money maker.

But had we taken it to the market, after much use, we would have discovered lots of liver disease and we would have had to take it off the market after probably spending in excess of $100 million. In terms of the company, it was a big loss, but the potential loss in terms of side effects to the patients, litigation, etc., would have been much more.

Frank went to the team, who were quite downcast. One day they had been working on a potential winner, and now the project was cancelled. Here's what he said to them:

Look, first of all, I'm really very happy that the environment we have here is one where a technician can make an observation and a supervisor can pursue

that observation and come out with an answer, rather than ignore it. Secondly, as a research director, let me tell you the three things that are important to me. The most important thing is to come up with a compound that not only meets an unmet medical need, but also advances science. Second is a compound that fills an unmet medical need, and third is a compound that advances science.

Your work on this compound is in the third category. It advances science, because nobody knew that this type of compound would stimulate specific cells to ingest cholesterol. I bet you anything that somebody will figure out how to use this compound to do other things without the side effects of getting trapped in the liver. So, this is a significant contribution to science. The team ought to be congratulated. It also has saved the company a lot of money by discovering this now. It has also prevented potential side effects to patients.

I'm going to celebrate what others would consider a failure, but what for us is a significant success. I want you guys to tell me how much time you need to tidy up some experiments, etc., and write some papers. I want you to take that time to do that before you get your next assignment.

Frank's message created a whole different atmosphere. They were relieved and feeling better about themselves. Of course, they were still feeling sad, but what they knew is that the administration did not see them as failures. Frank made a point of publicly recognizing them for their contribution:

I think when you do that in the environment, then people don't worry about failing and you begin to create an environment in which they are likely to make breakthroughs.

As noted, in the mid-1970s, I taught a large number of workshops on job burnout—the complete mental, emotional, and physical exhaustion that stems from an erosion of our energy over a long period of time. The most frequent cause of burnout mentioned was "all this energy poured into a black hole of work, with absoutely no sense of satisfactory results."

In changing market and technology conditions, many of our performance goals can be outside our control to achieve. Yet all of our performance appraisal and reward systems are based on achieving prescribed results. To advance in QQ, rewarding learning and even intelligent failure must be part of the formula.

There's the old cartoon of Charlie Brown bemoaning his first "A" on a school report card. When Lucy asked him why he was so distraught, he said, "There's no greater burden than high expectations!" This, of course, is the dilemma of sales people and others working against quotas or targets: The reward for hitting the mark is a higher mark the next time. (When the rewards are not also raised, this can lower morale, reduce the inspiration for superceding the mark, etc.)

With the combination of performance goals that are beyond our total control to achieve and the old childhood messages that reinforced that measurements were how we got caught doing less than we could, it's no wonder that people often resist being measured by their performance. We don't like having high expectations and then find out that "We just weren't good enough (again?)!"

How much we need to look outside of ourselves for positive feedback about our work is a good measure of our self-esteem. Feedback can give rise in us to two fears: "getting caught" and (surprisingly enough) "succeeding." Yet, feedback is necessary to know when to celebrate, having the chance to let ourselves know that we've been successful.

In the Challenge stage of the QQ process, we can try to ensure that the goal is meaningful and attainable by monitoring the business environment, assessing competitive position, and determining customer needs. We can then use that information throughout the Creative Journey to guide our progress toward a solution that has a reasonable probability of success.

For Frank Douglas:

> *To get people predisposed to making the leaps, I have found it extremely important to articulate a vision, or strategic intent, and to make them part of that process. It needs to be their vision, their strategic intent. The second thing I found important is to focus on the competition. To say I want to be the best is nice, but if you identify who is the best, who does what the best, then you can define the benchmarks.*
>
> *What we're about is getting people to work on things that are meaningful. We don't want you to spend five, six years working on a compound and then find we can't market it. We will have wasted your time. So we are concerned about making sure you use your talent and are fulfilled at the end of that time period because you were working on the right ideas and projects.*

To aim the efforts and careers of his research staff toward high satisfaction and success, Frank emphasizes the need to really understand customer's needs, where the customer is not only the patient but also the physician. In multidisciplinary teams, a discussion of "How should we differentiate the product?" begins to get people's juices flowing.

But more than that, Frank puts an even greater emphasis on understanding the status of competitors in their technology development and potential play in the marketplace:

We use the competition to create stretch. Initially, it is harder for researchers to focus on the competition than the customer, because focusing on the customer is nebulous—it's long-term, and people can pretend they're doing it when they're really not. When focusing on the competition, you can look at patents, data, publications, and assess where the competition is.

And it's not a judgment on what you have been doing to date, whether you have been good or bad, but rather, it enables you and the organization to work on meaningful projects. I tell my staff, "We know how difficult it is for you to give up your favorite project. If you have information that some approach either will not work or will be a very late entry to market, then the work will be for naught. You, yourself, I'm sure, will be happier to work on something that will have more meaning for you."

If we're not successful, what then? We saw in Chapter One how Frank Carrubba had to introduce the notion of intelligent failure to open up the atmosphere for risk taking and to stay on the edge of technology development. If we're not learning we can't innovate. Learning and innovating are the inhaling and exhaling of Quantum Quality. Intelligent failure is but one-half of the larger notion of learning from successes as well as failures.

At Hewlett-Packard, teams are often interviewed on video about what contributed to the quality of results they achieved. A core group studies the lessons learned and edits the videos to demonstrate key insights that might be transferred to other project teams, especially new ones. This focus on transferble insights is but one aspect of a full measurement system for innovativeness and Quantum Quality.

There are actually three levels of appraisal for QQ as described in the following.

Deliverables

This is the degree to which the actual goal-targeted output from a person or team—a proposal or report, a new chemical compound, a work systems improvement, or whatever—shows evidence of an innovative solution to a QQ challenge. As an example, listed in what follows are some "evidences" of innovative outputs from DowElanco researchers—weed management and herbicide biochemists, herbicide and formulation chemists, and lab management:

Biochemists

- Develop a new isolation procedure for an enzyme
- Isolate new enzymes
- Write project reports
- Write quarterly summaries on areas of innovation
- Identify new pesticide target sites and follow up to validation (or invalidation)
- Coordinate necessary test steps *to save time* in the evaluation of lead potential
- Decide to terminate an unproductive line of work

Chemists

- Develop a new synthetic method to arrive at a novel compound
- Prepare proprietary technology—patents
- Write for technical publications
- Evaluate whether we should continue to look at new technology from the results of feasibility testing
- Establish obtainable goals smaller than "product to market"
- Come up with a new area of herbicidal chemistry

Management

- Benchmark each formulation developed against the competition in terms of innovation
- Describe innovative work practices that have been improved
- Prepare patents/invention disclosures

Activities

This is the degree to which the person engages in the activities that heighten the odds that something innovative will occur—such as increasing the number of suggestions submitted, learning how to facilitate brainstorming sessions, and networking with professional colleagues at conferences. These are pieces of "evidence" of innovative activities for the DowElanco biochemists, chemists, and management.

Biochemists

- Schedule cross-functional meetings for exchange of knowledge within the company
- Set up meetings where we could discuss our innovations or where others could bring up how we were being innovative, as a cheerleading mechanism
- Spend time with peers—both internal and external (conferences, courses)
- Devote a small percentage of my time to work on a project of my own for which I am responsible to no one
- Spend a "week" at a library at a large university to think and put together a plan of research

Chemists

- Read current literature, spend some quiet time, and write proposals
- Spend more blue sky time and set aside time
- Perform patent searches in your area of interest
- Spend time at a retreat
- Attend conferences and scientific meetings
- Assemble customer focus groups
- Visit vendors
- Visit equipment vendors to test new equipment applicability to new products/processes
- Visit farmers to ask of their needs and for food group suggestions
- Allow time for "skunkworks" projects

Management

- Set up team training in innovation (styles/processes)
- Begin a group activity focused on innovating further the process of formulation development
- Devote 5–10 percent of my time to freelance innovative time/focus

Transferable Insights

This is the degree to which a person or team produces "sidebar" innovations, which helped to achieve the goal targeted deliverable but were not necessarily planned—such as developing a customer segmentation scheme while creating a new marketing strategy. (Most often they are sidebar innovations that occur in the midst of striving to meet the goal.

For example, a researcher might develop a new experimental design while studying a set of compounds; the molecular behavior was his/her goal, and the experimental design was a sidebar innovation—one that gives evidence of innovativeness and a transferable insight that could be valuable to others. Finally, here are some DowElanco examples of transferable insights.

Biochemist

- New enzyme isolation procedures
- Novel format for project proposal presentations
- Biorational design of enzyme inhibitors even if the inhibitor fails as a herbicide
- New test to show activity of a molecule/chemistry
- New way to organize data and see trends
- Budget for high-risk research with expectation of a certain percentage of failures; funds distributed by proposal review or by line item to departments

Chemists

- Evaluating a technology that might fail for one project but may have an application in another project
- New process for determining what formulation type and equipment should be made/evaluated for new products
- New screening tests for dispersing agents and wetting agents for new products

Management

- Documenting new ways for interfacing with other groups (customer/ marketing) to identify the product attributes and *validate* them
- Developing cross-functional team approaches and showcase their success

- Showcasing the use of experimental design for formulation development and its impact

It was this realm of Transferable Insights that Frank rewarded his research team, as described in the story at the start of this chapter.

All three demonstrate the innovativeness inherent in QQ. Learning is directly connected to the third QQ appraisal, Transferable Insights. Learning is of value to a group when the insights and lessons are transferable to other people or other situations. These learnings are rarely the main deliverable or goal for a project. Transferable Insights allows for defining a project to be successful in one way whether or not the project goal is fully achieved. If we focus only on deliverables, people will tend to set goals that are more easily attainable, because failure is not something we like to set up for ourselves, especially when there are financial, professional, and security consequences.

Linda Smith, vice president at Heller Financial, who you met in Chapter Three, has a clear point of view about setting up a tolerance for risk:

> *I do believe that you have to create an environment where change is ok. It's ok to make mistakes. If you make a mistake, mop it up and move on. And the more people are able to do that and not get a dressing down because of it, the more willing they are to take those chances and to accept change as a way of life. What we're trying to create here is an environment where change is normal.*
>
> *I have a whole new perspective on performance reviews and in fact I'm on the executive committee for our company that's going to be reviewing the entire performance appraisal system. My philosophy on performance reviews is that you don't talk negative. If there is one area that you want an employee to develop, you never go beyond one area. Everything in that performance review should be positive because there is nothing more debilitating than a performance review that has many negatives; instead, you talk to them about it before the performance review. People want to be good at what they do. They don't want to fail.*

Appraisal cannot be only in relation to our own efforts and achievements internally. They have greater meaning in terms of the impact on stakeholders. Often, we tend to look at measurement mainly for the individual's contribution. Yet, so few results can be attributed anymore to the effort of a single person. Teams are the locus of power and performance.

The title of this chapter is "Reward Focused Learning as Well as Improvement." We've looked at focused learning (transferable insights) and achievements (deliverables). How do we reward teams as well as individuals for their performance relative to QQ?

There are ten major catgories of satisfactions and rewards for Quantum Quality and innovation:

Self-determination and autonomy

Advancement and promotions

Training and development

Intrinsically satisfying assignments

Social interaction with mentors and key peers

Financial rewards

Impact on valued stakeholders

Environment in work areas

Recognition, public and private

Security of job and career

Some are oriented more toward intrinsic motivation. Some are more extrinsic. In research I conducted at Pillsbury in 1987, with the brand managers of the US Foods Division, there was a correlation between four SATISFIERS elements: self-determination, intrinsic, training, and private recognition. There was an inverse correlation to these among three others: advancement, financial rewards, and public recognition. These groups are distinguished in that the former are more intrinsic in the value placed on them, whereas the satisfaction is experienced independently of others' notice or involvement. The latter are extrinsic, where it takes someone outside the performer to help provide the sense of satisfaction.

Curiously, over the past two decades, many research studies have shown that greater creativity is fostered in people when the task has intrinsic, natural motivation. For most people, having a personally meaningful goal is a much more powerful driver than extrinsic rewards. When we pursue an important goal yet stay unattached to the outcome—when the process of our journey is as important as arriving at our destination—we often have more access to our flexibility and wisdom. We also persevere longer, even when no one is looking to reward our behavior.

The key to celebrating results is much more than hurrahs and yahoos. We have many cultural inhibitors against praising ourselves, even if we feel proud of our accomplishments. In part, this is based on the wisdom that, at some level, we as individuals or small teams were not fully responsible or in control of producing the results. We are part of something larger that had direct influence on the outcome. This larger whole could be the department, the company, the community, the country, the international market, or even something more spiritual.

In this light, the deepest sense of completion—the true essence of emotionally completing a QQ project—is the opportunity to express *gratitude*, to say, *Thank You*. This reconnects us through the heart to the larger whole, who contributed to the achievement as well as the learning.

Strengthening the System

In additon to the factors detailed in the previous chapter—Resource Allocation and Transition Management—managers and team leaders can empower teams in the completion stage by aligning the teams on the factors of Impact Appraisal and Satisfaction/Rewards.

One key to empowering quality teams at this stage is evaluating the impact of both individuals and teams for their level of achievements and shared learning. The other is carefully providing both intrinsic and extrinsic levels of rewards and satisfactions.

O. *Impact Appraisal.* This is the degree to which the team knows how and when its results will be appraised, with success based on learnings as well as achievements. When this is done well, the team knows how and when its performance will be appraised, for tangible "deliverables," activities that foster innovation, and transferable insights/ learning; the team members are acknowledged by sponsors for both individual and group performance upon the achievement of milestones.

P. *Satisfaction/Rewards.* This is the degree to which the team receives from its sponsors the types of satisfaction and rewards that are most gratifying for its efforts and results. When this is done well, the team receives both *extrinsic* rewards[1] and *intrinsic* rewards[2] for its tangible accomplishments and for the learning and knowledge it generates, understanding that unsuccessful performance will be acknowledged but not

---

[1] Such as money, promotions, and public recognition.
[2] Such as autonomy, time off, project selection, and professional development opportunities.

punished; the team members are rewarded both individually and col-
lectively.

As sponsors and teams align on these two issues, they will foster a culture
in which they appraise and gain satisfaction for both learning and
improvement. Customer-feedback systems (e.g., point of sale), 360-degree
performance appraisal, and electronic performance-recognition systems
are some of the tools that can help institutionalize this aspect of a positive
sponsor-team relationship.

Practicing the Paradigm

Learning

The key question that stimulates and organizes learning in the
Completion stage is, "What's working?," which includes not only "What
appraisal process do we use?," but also "What satisfactions do we
receive?" Chapter Ten stated that in asking, "What appraisal process do
we use?" We must learn how to:

(N) have access to sufficient financial, human, time, resources
(O) participate in planning and implementing organizational change

For "What satisfactions do we receive?," we must learn about

(P) giving and receiving feedback on individual, team, and organizational
  achievements and learnings
(Q) sustaining motivation through intrinsic and extrinsic sources of satisfaction

Although we often fear to give or receive feedback, the key to having the
experience of success and completion is learning how to do this in a way
that heightens our sense of motivation, self-competence, initiative, and
self-corrective growth. And learning about the individual patterns of
intrinsic and extrinsic satisfaction needs to be driven by much more than
"reinforcing postitive behavior." Rather than focusing on benefits and
"what's in it for me" patterns, Quantum Quality bases feedback and satisfaction on fulfillment of purpose, with a clear expression of gratitude at

the conribution of others. This creates a truly organic (rather than mechanistic) process of spiraling competence, knowledge, and performance for success.

To give ourselves the insights we need to participate in this giving and receiving process, we can inquire, "To what extent do I feel self-secure versus vulnerable when my performance is being appraised?" Or "How do I assert myself to help provide the most important intrinsic and extrinsic satisfactions of my colleagues and myself?" The answers to these questions complete the cycle started with setting the most motivating goals in the Challenge stage, leading us to higher levels of motivation, meaning, risk taking, and initiative. They support our ongoing commitment to the new paradigm and mind-set of Quantum Quality, where we can feel and say to ourselves, "We celebrate our own and others' success!"

Values

Right Action shows up as respect for the contribution we and others make to achieve meaningful goals and learnings. Do we acknowledge learning and achievements with true gratitude? Do we even take the time to measure results, to even have the chance to acknowledge success?

So many ways of rewarding people are really manipulation schemes in (partial) disguise. As behavioral reinforcement systems, they are an extension of the "people are part of the machinery" way of thinking. When people sense that bonuses, recognition, etc., have no real heart in them, the process becomes just another system to figure out and "beat" (creatively). However, when there is a sincere thankfulness that demonstrates the respect of one human for another, for their contribution and effort, then even the simplest acknowledgments take on a vast power to build spirit and renew energy.

Creativity

Many studies have shown that the level of creativity in young and old goes up when they are working for intrinsic satisfaction rather than external reward. It's as if the external rewards introduce the judgmental mind to evaluate and censor ideas, trying to meet the expectations of the external rewarder.

How does this fit with most corporate reward systems, which emphasize extrinsic recognition, promotions, etc.? It's a paradox that working without desiring the fruits of our work—to aim true, work hard, and not be attached to what happens—may be the greatest key to Quantum Quality success!

Sustainability

Given the enormity of succeeding in meeting the needs of employees, customers, society, and the environment, we might find ourselves asking, "What's in it for me to take on such challenges?" That may sound like a reasonable enough question (in the current paradigm of thinking), but it's not the right question to be asking, for it focuses on personal benefits. Sustainability demands that we go beyond thinking just about personal benefits, to see motivation in terms of *expressing and fulfilling one's purpose.*

As people, we have a tendency to think in circles and rehash old information unless something intervenes: either a crisis or new learning. If a crisis intervenes, then we'll do things differently. Or we can choose to avoid the crisis by learning. The choice is ours.

Sometimes, in the mystery of being human, we choose the hard road. We have to be willing to look at the world in entirely new ways. This is easier said than done. As Frank Douglas concludes:

> *You cannot expect people who have worked with a particular paradigm to suddenly discover a new paradigm. You have to lead in nontraditional ways. You have to take them out of their environment, put them into different environments, give them glimpses of themselves doing things differently, but in a way that they can see some relevance to what they do. Expand the mind.*

Yet to create a sustainable future for ourselves, our children's children, and our planet, we must expand our minds, and our hearts.

PART 3

The Essence of
Quantum Quality

12

Putting Our Deepest Values to Work

We don't need to look over people's shoulders and make sure they do what they're supposed to be doing. People want to do more than what they're being allowed to do. When we restructured the organization, focused people on the work processes, and helped them learn what they were capable of doing individually and as a group, the impact was incredible.

—Chris Ehlers, transportation operations manager, Procter & Gamble

Our quality of life always has been, and will be, based on our understanding and ability to translate the deepest longings of the human spirit into reality. The game of business is how to turn wishes into reality. Can we bring these two paths together? Can we take in some fresh insights and "inspire" our businesses and societies toward economic and social transformation? For many, many people, the answer is a very practical, tangible, resounding "Yes!"

Our commitment and effectiveness at work is tied to exercising our deepest personal values. For example, Chris Ehlers and his colleagues at Procter & Gamble's Pampers operations had the opportunity to put their personal values to work on a multimillion dollar startup for a Pampers (disposable diapers) operation for the Japanese market, to be situated in their Oxnard, California, plant.

The plant manager decided he was going to try a new approach to startup. Normally, they would bring in busloads of process engineers and professional managers to check out the equipment, set it up, get it started, run it until they got good product, and then train the technicians. He believed that we could do it better if we had fewer managers and involved the people who were actually going to run it.

So there were only five managers and nine technicians. They did their own hiring, set up their own teams, checked out the equipment, brought it in, and set it up. A normal startup curve from the day you start making product till you reach the full, ongoing rate is two years. They did it in eight months. And for the first time in the history of the company, a project came in $2 million under budget.

The team experienced a great sense of community and ownership for their work, born out of their personal values. That feeling was tested a year later, when the Japanese market went flat and there was too much capacity. A decision was made to shut down that part of the plant even though by that time they were outrunning the rest of the division in all measures.

The group decided they wanted to have the best shutdown ever. Normally, we'd break the line into hundreds of components, box them up, and ship them over to wherever they would put it back together. The problem is that we knew the historical startup curve for once-started equipment—disassembled and reassembled—was almost four years.

They said there's got to be a better way to do this. One of them jokingly said we ought to simply bolt the sucker to something and break it into fewer components. They measured the line and found that they could break it into four major components. So they put railroad rails under the line and with high-speed carbide bits drilled all the way through the support beams. They bolted the line, broke it into four major components, put them into huge sea tankers, and shipped them to Saudi Arabia. Six months after they arrived and were put in, they were ongoing.

It saved tens of millions of dollars to the company. It's because they had so much ownership that they weren't willing to have people come back and say, "You may have done a great job of starting up, but you didn't do a very good job of shutting down." We didn't have any preconceived notions about what they should and shouldn't do, so they were allowed to innovate freely.

Another factor was that they all knew they'd have jobs, and that the majority of the management staff was going to be integrated into other plant operations. However, they didn't fully know just how rich and expansive the experience had been until much later.

Interestingly enough, within five years, all the leadership positions in the plant were filled by former Pampers people.

What do we mean by deepest personal values? A few years ago, members of the Corporate Innovation Committee of 3M Corporation asked me to make a presentation to them on "Innovative Corporate Cultures." At the time, I was in charge of the Innovation Management Program at SRI (Stanford Research Institute) International, an international "think tank" and consulting firm.

At the end, the 3M representative who brought me in, Bob Gubrud, saw a book in my briefcase as I was packing. It had a faded gold cross on it.

"What are you reading, William?" he asked.

"Oh, it's a book about six saints from the thirteenth to sixteenth centuries." That's all I planned to say, being reluctant to talk about spiritual matters with my clients.

"What prompts your interest in that—religious conviction, curiosity, philosophy?"

"Well, to tell the truth, for a few years now I've realized that a major theme in my life and work has been, "How might creativity, business and spiritual values somehow be facets of the same diamond rather than separate subjects?"

"That's amazing. That's exactly what's been on my mind the past six months! Let's get a bite to eat and talk about that."

And so we did. We discussed how creativity encompassed how we expressed our unique individuality as well as how we responded to work challenges—how business included any organization involved in an "exchange of value," whether they be profit enterprises, government, education, or nonprofit institutions—how spiritual values were the same as the most fundamental human values, which bring out the best in people of all cultures.

These intrinsic human values—such as well-being, truth, inner peace, right conduct, and love—directly support established business values, such as service, communication, creativity, responsibility, and excellence. They are part and parcel of achieving quantum leaps in process improvement, customer impact, and personal commitment.

Can you emphasize such values and still run a successful business? For Dick Eppel, the answer is a resounding, "Yes!" Dick was general manager of a communication systems division of a major electronics corporation. He took that job with the assignment of turning the division around.

It was definitely a division in serious trouble, a result of too much success in their marketing activities without enough forethought for how they were going to execute that successfully. Clearly, one goal had to be to satisfy the customer. And the second thing was to get the people to believe that there was a recovery possible here.

We set up a prioritization of what customers we were going to satisfy when, with the goal that we were going to satisfy all customers. We would not take on any more business whatsoever that would jeopardize satisfying our current customers. That was to convince the employees that we weren't asking impossible things of them.

Everything had to be credible—the roadmap, the vision, the how-you're going-to-get-there—all had to be credible. I was the one who had to say, "No." I was the one who had to say, "Trust me." I was the one who had to say, "Once we get through this, then we are all going to win."

One time, a salesman came to Dick with a potential new customer who wanted a delivery date that he knew they couldn't meet. The salesman wanted an exception to their strategy so he could get the sale.

I hung tough on not accepting business that we couldn't deliver on. That was a test. I would talk to a customer, look him in the eye, and say, "Do you want me to lie to you?" I used words that had an emotional impact, but there was no ambiguity. They accepted that. It turned out that we could execute good business, deliver on that business, and manage it to a schedule, even though there were threats of going someplace else or walking away from it.

After two years, things were significantly improved. Turnover was down. We got the division to break even, or pretty close to break even. Every contract got delivered on. Every contract. The most important piece that we saved has represented about $13–20 million per year of cash-rich profits ever since.

What did it take for Dick and his division to succeed? He named two things beyond having the right strategy:

One was a sense of positive perseverance: positive expectations, positive visualization. That had a lot to do with the result.

The second thing was that the management team—the people and myself—for one reason or another, amalgamated in a way that was very unique to me. I've always enjoyed working with people, always felt like I had good teams to work with. But in this operation, there was one other level that was a bonding beyond friendship and comraderie. There was just a sense of caring and a sense of concern. And I even use the words of "a genuine sense of love" between the parties, even though that was never expressed verbally.

Truth telling. Love. Business. They need each other: Truth and love enrich business success, and business is a way for love to express itself, serving people's needs. Why then are we so afraid at work to call it "love," when that's what it really is?

The entire QQ process, the Creative Journey, can become our means for enriching our sense of personal values put to work. In 1989, I read a book that has influenced me for years: *The Way to Shambhala*.[1] Edwin Bernbaum, the author, speaks of the journey we all take while living on this earth. From the Tibetan story of the spiritual quest of Shambala to the Greek mythical quest of Odysseus, there's a clear sequence we're taught about how to take on the challenges we face, whether the challenge be death, a relationship, or work.

The story line goes something like this:

You're on a quest, and you come to an impassable river (or some other obstacle), guarded by a demon.

The instructions are clear: Withdraw to prepare yourself and gather strength—identify with a Power (Divine) so its energies merge in you; then call forth the demon.

Do battle until you are victorious.

Having subdued/tamed the demon, it becomes an ally to get you across the impassable river; on the other side, take an account, with gratitude, of what you've gained to assist you on the next stage of your journey.

The most powerful insight for me in this was the step of empowerment in the face of the river and demon. This step is the essence of tapping into spiritual values and putting their power to work. As I now see it, there are four stages to handling any challenge that requires a new solution, and each stage has two steps that parallel the mythical journey (see Table 12.1).

In 1987, Lorna Catford and I cotaught the "Creativity in Business" course at Stanford University's Graduate School of Business. She aided me in making the link between this heroic journey (of teams as well as individuals) and the actual process of working creatively to handle challenges and improve quality. One day she showed how the creative process goes through a cycle of confidence and darkness. As I examined the stages of the creative process I had seen in my own work, the basic "confidence curve" of the Quantum Quality process became clear, as show in Figure 12.1.

---

[1] Edwin Bernbaum, *The Way to Shambhala* (Los Angeles: J P Tarcher, 1989).

TABLE 12.1

Stage	Steps	Journey
Challenge	Establish goal; meet uncertainty	"On a quest; come to impassable river and demon"
Focus	Tap into character; analyze issues	"Take on inner power; call forth the demon"
Creative solution	Generate options; decide on solution	"Do battle; defeat/tame demon"
Completion	Implement solution; celebrate results	"Get across impassable river; take account of gains"

It's often the plunge from confidence to darkness that grabs our attention the most—and that calls upon our deepest human values to create the empowerment we need. However, we have the opportunity—indeed, the need—to apply personal values throughout the *entire* process of dealing with our work challenges.

This empowered journey can be found in extraordinary or everyday work events. As a dramatic example, Edgar Mitchell once had a very different job from most of us: He is one of those very rare human beings who has had the privilege of walking on the moon's surface, as part of the Apollo XIV crew in 1971. His adventure can be told in terms of the four stages we've just covered. His personal values are evident each step of the way. And his experience in space led to the spiritualization of those values—he returned a very different person.

The Challenge

The idea of an opportunity to explore this new environment and then go to the moon was virtually an irresistible challenge. I characterize the space flight, of getting off the planet, as being as significant an event as when the first sea creatures crawled out onto land. Here we human beings have left our native habitat and started to explore a totally alien environment. My passion for many years since childhood is how does the universe really work. I early on found disagreement between my scientific training and my religious training. I have been pursuing a resolution to the conflicts in cosmology ever since.

The Focus

I recognized very early in life that fear is to be overcome. If it is physical danger, by being skillful; if it's a psychological fear, then get into yourself and root it out.

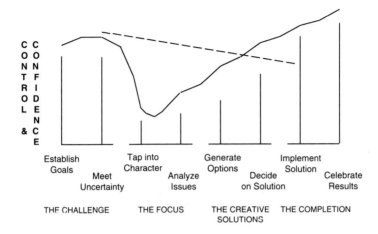

FIGURE 12.1.   The Creative Journey™

Preparation for the Apollo flight involved many skills. Piloting skills were important. And since we had to navigate on the lunar surface, there had to be a lot of muscle coordination, strength, and know-how. In addition, there was all the academic work . . . geology, orbital mechanics, rocket fuels, the particular computer systems of both spacecraft-command module and lunar module. So all that knowledge, that training, and those skills had to be practiced over and over again until we were at a point where it was automatic. Then we could use the human judgment factor to deal with surprises and unexpected events.

The Creative Solutions

There is always creativity, because almost never did the spacecraft fail in the ways that we had trained for. The most creative problem was before we went down to the lunar surface. The automatic abort system had somehow failed . . . in such as way that if we tried to descend to the surface, it would automatically switch on and take us back into orbit. This was less than two hours before we were to supposed to start down to the surface. Most of the time the spacecraft was behind the moon and out of communication with the earth. The computer was reprogrammed with the help of the ground, and we had just ten minutes to implement the solution after we came from behind the moon before the engines were to be ignited. We successfully did that with just a few seconds to spare by the way.

The Completion

Looking at the earth, the moon and the sun—this powerful experience of seeing earth and our whole solar system against the background of the cosmos—

had a very profound effect . . . an overwhelming sense of being connected with the universe, of feeling connected to all things, to the most distant galaxies, to earth, to self, to sun. The recognition is that our scientific description of the way the universe is put together was at best incomplete and perhaps in some ways inaccurate. The universe is more of a living organism than a set of discrete things. I had to shed and reevaluate much of my prior learning.

What did come out of that experience was an enormous sense of responsibility that goes with the power of creativity. We are creative individuals, and we each have to accept with our creative potential the responsibility that goes with that. The word responsibility means to accept one's choices and the consequences of those choices, becoming proactive rather than reactive.

And that means letting go of fear. Love is letting go of fear. That is precisely the experience when you leave fear behind. And with that comes the sense of responsiveness, or responsibility, that you take charge of your own life, let go of your fears. Automatically that brings this deeper sense of love and responsibility for one's self, surroundings, environment, and planet.

What does that have to do with the rest of us? The challenges we face go through the very same stages. And at each stage, we have the opportunity to put our deepest values to work. Willis Harman in *Global Mind Change*,[2] points out the opportunities—and the responsibilities—that business leaders and managers (at all levels!) face as we approach the dawn of the 21st century.

Leaders in world business are the first true planetary citizens. They have worldwide capability and responsibility; their domains transcend national boundaries. Their decisions affect not just economies, but societies; not just the direct concerns of business, but world problems of poverty, environment, and security. Up to now there has been no guiding ethic . . . no tradition of and no institutionalization of a philosophy capable of wisely guiding its shaping force. Such a new ethos for business may be in the process of forming.

World business will be a key actor in the ultimate resolution of the macroproblem. It crosses national boundaries with much more ease than do political institutions and the business corporation is a far more flexible and adaptive organization than the bureaucratic structures of governments.

---

[2] Willis Harman, *Global Mind Change* (Indianapolis IN: Knowledge Systems, Inc., 1988), p. 132.

Chris Ehlers relates one example of productively using work as a learning environment for peoples' personal and professional growth:

I was the manager of the organization called Outbound Operations. This transportation and support group managed $450 million of freight a year. To do that, they had the largest computer system in the company. And we had three full-time college-trained—in one case, masters-trained—people just to take care of the system. The people who were actually administering the system were all high school graduates. As part of this restructuring, they wanted to take responsibility for the system themselves. They didn't feel like they were getting the responsiveness from the professionals, who were more concerned about the language and programming than the applications.

We used a company to look at what people were capable of doing outside of their job experience. We had two people who were "lifelong learners," so we put them on the computer system. Within two years, one of those young ladies programmed in three languages, including Cobol. And they made more application changes to the system in two years than the professionals had done in the previous ten years.

I didn't tell them, "You can't do that." I said, "I'm willing to give you a chance to do that—if you have that capability." Rather than trying to find out what was wrong, and developing them according to some predetermined job model, we went out and asked, "What do they look like now? How do we build upon their capabilities? How do we match them up with the right place in the organization?"

We have to look at individual needs that we as an organization have and match them to individual capability, and that can become a ponderous process because in just P & G alone, we have some 90,000 people. How do you manage each of them individually? I don't think it's that difficult. In some cases, I think you don't manage them. You allow them to manage themselves.

Over the past ten years, I've had the wonderful opportunity to provide corporate consulting on creativity, innovation, and quality improvement in countries such as the United States, Canada, Japan, Australia, Singapore, Malaysia, the Netherlands, Great Britain, Bulgaria, Czechoslovakia, and the former Soviet Union. Although people in each culture are certainly different, deep down they are very much the same in their quest for a rich quality of life—spiritually, emotionally, and mentally as well as materially.

Yet, somehow, all around this planet, we've lost a basic feel for the deeper, more spiritual side of this richness. We've lost touch with how our work contribution can be an exercise of our deepest values, and a training ground for discovering more of who we are as spiritual/human beings. By focusing so much on material growth, we actually miss the very basis of healthy, economic prosperity—giving our best to enrich our surroundings, our environment, and our planet.

Vaslav Havel said in his inaugural address as president of Czechoslovakia, "We have been lied to a great deal, and I don't presume you elected me to lie to you more. We are a morally ill country." He went on to say that unless they learned to be truthful, open, and respectful with each other, they would never succeed in rebuilding the economy and country.

> *If a better economic and political model is to be created, then perhaps more than ever before it must derive from profound existential and moral changes in society.*

This was an extension of what he wrote in the late 1970s:

> *If a better economic and political model is to be created, then perhaps more than ever before it must derive from profound existential and moral changes in society. This is not something that can be designed and introduced like a new car. If it is to be more than just a new variation on the old degeneration, it must above all be an expression of life in the process of transforming itself.*
>
> *A better system will not automatically ensure a better life. In fact, the opposite is now true: Only by creating a better life can a better system be developed.*

We in the west are in the same boat. It's just easier to see in the black-and-white need for renewal of the eastern European countries. We face the same need, the same call. To create this better life, we can't wait for the system to change. The system will change as a result of creating this better life. Our powers to affect the environment and the well-being of people all over the planet make this spiritual renewal absolutely critical to our economic and social health.

As Havel embodies, there is a widespread awakening to the importance of bringing our deepest values into our work, to make a better contribution to others' well-being while fostering our own personal growth.

Native people throughout the world refer to the earth as "Mother," the very embodiment of love and caring. Their relationship with life was, is, so personal! They live and work very differently, based on a sense of connection rather than an alienated "me-versus-them" world view. Imagine the frame of mind it takes to poison our own mother, yet so many business decisions do just that! And how do we ever grow a healthy economy and a wealthy quality of life based on an overly analytical, discon-nected mind-set?

Personal and economic renewal depends on our return to feeling that the universe is alive, not a dead machine. Sartre and other existentialists often stated that, as human beings, we have been thrown into a meaning-less universe, "condemned to be free" and to use our intellect to create our own meaning out of chaos. By contrast, Alan Watts once mused that just as a tree grows leaves, the universe grows people: that perhaps instead of "being thrown into the universe," we have grown out of it, an integral part of Creation, sharing in its powers of creativity and love.

Fred Schwettman of Hewlett-Packard (who you met in Chapter One) related to me:

We had a discussion one time about values and beliefs in our staff meeting. I think one of the most important things we could do is to really articulate what our personal purpose is—really trying to understand what we're doing to grow and to work on that. An example could be to know God or to find love associated with God and to practice that in whatever I do. One woman said, "I need the money to eat and to pay the rent." If her purpose is to make enough money to have a good living, then that's a good purpose.

But if we're not accomplishing something here that's really important to your basic reason for existence—if "doing a good job" is your personal pur-pose in life—perhaps you haven't really thought about it a lot.

As time goes on, my purpose turns more and more spiritual and maybe that's because you either get wiser or you get closer to the end of your life. What can I contribute to people's lives? I also have to spend my time trying to figure out how we'll survive within this industry, which is horribly com-petitive. You can practice honesty, integrity and caring, and all of those things, but at the same time, this is a tremendously competitive environ-ment. But overall, it's like when the time comes to check out, you better feel really good about what you accomplished and making a little profit here and there is probably not going to cut it.

Equally as direct was Chris Ehlers, stating what so many other people have expressed to me:

I'm a very spiritually centered person. I try to relate to everything through my values as a Christian. Take, for instance, the role model of Christ as a leader: He was a servant to those whom he led. That's what I feel I have to be.

I feel the problem with business today is that it doesn't look at things holistically. If we see things as totally independent of each other, then any-

thing we do is okay so long as it adds to our bottom line. My religious values say that there is more to life than the bottom line. I am accountable for my actions throughout eternity. Therefore, regardless of the short-term rewards, I try to consider the impact of my actions on everything around me. Our approach to the environment is a good example of this lack of interdependent thinking. We have yet to make the connection between the reforestation process, the hydration process, and the sustainability of life on earth. All of these things are interconnected, but we treat them as separate entities. The same is true in business. We do not look at the long-term impact of our actions on the people, places, and things around us.

The problem with changing this perspective is that we are stuck in a paradigm. One thing I have learned is that you can't evolve out of a paradigm, you have to break out of it. This requires an intervention. Water can sit forever and it will not boil until an intervention is made in the form of heat. Once you apply enough heat, a quantum change occurs and the water boils— thus changing into steam. Until leaders are willing to make an intervention of this sort, there will be no quantum change in business.

Living with well-being, truth, peace, right action, and love can become quite natural. These deepest human values may be labeled differently among people and yet have a common heritage in our humanity—beyond cultural and personal differences. People everywhere are finding new openings within themselves for putting these deepest values to work.

Bob Galvin, chairman of the executive committee to the board of directors for Motorola—the man most responsible for leading Motorola's growth over the last 30 years—recently addressed 30 of his vice presidents and officers. He stated that the company's success has been due to its always taking the minority direction, away from the crowd. Their job, he said, was to become role models in creatively seeing and doings things differently— being "dazzling" thinkers —and in building a new culture of collaboration.

He went on to say that the key to their job description was to spread hope, build trust, and inspire acts of faith ("Things are do-able that are not necessarily proveable.") As a bottom line, he suggested, "Faith, Hope, and Trust. . . . Theology is very practical business." And when asked how these values relate to the "real world of business," he replied that one has to become more than a good technical or financial person. To him, success in the real world required faith, hope, and trust.

We can be ourselves and live these values. As part of the "two-way street" of work, we can develop our deepest values as well as our talents through QQ, as we make a significant contribution to their internal and external customers. As we face big and little challenges, we can ennoble our work by responding from the deepest part of ourselves and our values.

The search for meaning must ultimately go beyond how we acquire things and experiences. The focus on making valuable contributions to society is what drives personal and social prosperity. It means learning from history's spiritual leaders, to find in ourselves what they embodied. As stated in India by the spiritual leader Sai Baba, "Not until man learns to value mankind will anything else find its proper value."

This value, this meaning, can be found amidst the creative expression of our minds, hearts, and souls. With a mastery of the external factors and a commitment to personal growth we will be living models of continuous learning and improvement.

It may take a tremendous amount of courage—literally, "heartfulness"—and we may have to buck the backcurrents of self-centered business practices. However, through Quantum Quality, we can develop and practice the learning, values, creativity, and sustainability it takes to succeed in the 1990s. May the quality of our work always reflect the highest quality of our souls.

ABOUT THE AUTHOR

William C. Miller is president of the Global Creativity Corporation. He is author of *The Creative Edge: Fostering Innovation Where You Work*, which topped the business best-seller list for independent bookstores in 1987, and *Creativity: The Eight Master Keys*, the first training package ever recommended by *Fortune* magazine.

From 1983 to 1987, he was senior management consultant for the Innovation Management program at SRI International (formerly Stanford Research Institute). Prior to joining SRI, he was director of training and development for Victor Equipment Company, the leading American manufacturer of gas welding equipment. Mr. Miller specialized in math and physics in addition to his psychology major at Stanford University. His M.A. from West Georgia College emphasized organization development.

Mr. Miller assists executives and professionals to discover the deeper values that drive their most creative work and to enhance their skills in producing innovations within their organizational environment. His work has two primary focuses: optimizing the culture for creativity and innovation and finding innovative solutions to specific business problems.

He works primarily with Fortune 500 corporations and multinationals such as 3M, Hewlett-Packard, Procter & Gamble, IBM, Eli Lilly, DuPont, Levi Strauss, Conoco Oil, and Pillsbury. He has also taught the "Creativity in Business" course at Stanford University's Graduate School of Business.

Mr. Miller's other publications include:

- "Synergizing Total Quality and Innovation" (with N. Terry Pearce), *The National Productivity Review* (Winter/Spring 1988).

- "The Strategic Innovation Management Assessment Profile," in *New Directions in Creative and Innovative Management* (ed. by Yuji Ijiri and Robert Kuhn).

- "How Well Do We Put Our Spiritual Values to Work?" in *New Traditions in Business* (ed. by John Renesch).

Index